Investing with Keynes

Praise for *Investing with Keynes*

'An outstanding intellectual biography of John Maynard Keynes, illuminating the world of one of the most captivating intellects of the twentieth century and his transformative ideas.'

Gautam Baid, author of *The Joys of Compounding*

'A fascinating account of Keynes's career as an investor. It shows very well the link between Keynes's experience as an investor, speculating on the markets, and his theory. As an investor Keynes became more and more aware of the market's uncertainty and volatility.'

Lord Robert Skidelsky, author of *Keynes: The Return of the Master*

'Provides an opportunity to reflect on what made Mr Keynes also arguably the most astute observer of the investment game that ever lived.'

Financial Times

'Fascinating – what the managers of endowment funds can learn from Keynes doing the same job.'

Marc Andreessen, venture capitalist and entrepreneur

Investing with Keynes

HOW THE WORLD'S GREATEST ECONOMIST OVERTURNED CONVENTIONAL WISDOM AND MADE A FORTUNE ON THE STOCK MARKET

JUSTYN WALSH

HARPER
BUSINESS
An Imprint of HarperCollins *Publishers*

First published in 2021 by Black Inc.,
An imprint of Schwartz Books Pty Ltd, Australia

This edition published in India in 2021 by Harper Business
An imprint of HarperCollins *Publishers*
A-75, Sector 57, Noida, Uttar Pradesh 201301, India
www.harpercollins.co.in

2 4 6 8 10 9 7 5 3 1

Originally published as *Keynes and the Market* by Wiley, Hoboken, NJ in 2008
This edition published in 2021

P-ISBN: 978-93-5422-413-3
E-ISBN: 978-93-5422-416-4

Printed and bound at
Replika Press Pvt. Ltd.

MIX
Paper from responsible sources
FSC® C016779

This book is produced from independently certified FSC® paper to ensure responsible forest management.

CONTENTS

For Joe, Tom, Dan & Ada

INTRODUCTION

JOHN MAYNARD KEYNES CONFERRED a distinct glamor on the dismal science of economics. He was a Cambridge don, key member of the Bloomsbury set, best-selling author, husband of a world-famous ballerina, father of modern macroeconomics, valued government adviser, ennobled member of the House of Lords, and midwife to the IMF and the World Bank. His bracing response to the doldrums of the Great Depression – "The patient needs exercise, not rest" – heralded the Keynesian era of managed capitalism and pump-primed Western economies. Renowned almost as much for the variability of his opinions as for the vigor, style, and intelligence with which they were advanced, Keynes delighted in assaulting conventional wisdom and deployed pungent prose as his weapon of choice.

Despite affecting an aristocratic disdain for the profession of money- making, Keynes was also an incredibly successful stock market investor. At the time of his death, his net worth – largely accrued through his investment activities and supplemented by judicious art purchases – amounted to the present-day equivalent of $30 million. The Cambridge college fund administered by Keynes recorded a twelve-fold increase in its value while under his stewardship, a period during which the broader market averages failed even to double. In his role as chairman of one of Britain's most venerable life assurance companies his speeches were, according to a journalist at the time, "so highly regarded by the City that his prediction of a trend was enough to jiggle the stock market." Keynes was that rarest of beasts – an economist who, having clambered down from his ivory tower, mastered the financial markets in practice as well as in theory.

Notwithstanding his financial success, one might reasonably query how an analysis of Keynes' stock market techniques can profit the modern investor. Keynes was, after all, a child of the Victorian era and died three-quarters of a century ago. He lived in a different, more decorous time than our own – Keynes could have been describing himself when he conjured the image of "the inhabitant of London . . . sipping his morning tea in bed," languidly contemplating whether to "adventure his wealth in the . . . new enterprises of any quarter of the world." He invested in whaling companies and other now-defunct industries, and was directed by editors to ensure that his magazine articles were of sufficient length to allow readers to work through at least three glasses of port. Redolent as he is of another age, is there anything to be gained from an appraisal of Keynes' investment principles in this era of day traders, delta ratios, and dot-coms?

The answer, perhaps surprisingly, is a resounding "yes". After a couple of false starts, Keynes alighted on a set of precepts that won him singular stock market success. In the twilight of his long investment career, he declared with characteristic immodesty that:

> the financial concerns where I have had my own way have been uniformly prosperous . . . My difficulties in financial quarters all through have been the difficulty of getting unorthodox advice accepted by others concerned.

These unorthodox tenets anticipated, to a remarkable degree, the investment philosophies of some conspicuously successful contemporary "value investors," most notably Warren Buffett of Berkshire Hathaway. Noting that Keynes' "brilliance as a practicing investor matched his brilliance in thought," Buffett has on a number of occasions recognized his intellectual allegiance to the English economist. Just as importantly to the modern reader, Keynes' observations were set out in the limpid, casually elegant language for which he was rightly acclaimed. As his friend, the newspaper baron Lord Beaverbrook, noted, Keynes made "exciting literature out of finance" – truly a colossal feat.

Keynes wrote in his best-known work *The General Theory of Employment, Interest and Money* that:

> practical men, who believe themselves to be quite exempt from any intellectual influences, are usually the slaves of some defunct economist. Madmen in authority, who hear voices in the air, are distilling their frenzy from some academic scribbler of a few years back.

Following the Global Financial Crisis of 2008 and more recently the worldwide disruption wreaked by the COVID-19 pandemic, Keynes' academic scribblings have once again become the dominant creed for Western nations scrambling to kickstart moribund economies. Paralleling this Keynesian renaissance are advances in the field of behavioral finance validating the economist's observations on investor psychology and stock market dynamics, while recent empirical studies affirm Keynes' reputation as an expert stock picker and star fund manager. The insights of John Maynard Keynes – a man who lived and prospered through two world wars, the Crash of 1929, and the Great Depression – are more relevant than ever in our era of profound uncertainty and volatility.

Keynes' upbringing and personal philosophy deeply influenced his attitude toward money and its pursuit. Any investigation of the man's investment principles must, therefore, also chart some of the key landmarks of his life. One of Keynes' closest friends, the iconoclastic Lytton Strachey, remarked that his professional task as a biographer was to:

> row out over that great ocean of material, and lower down into it, here and there, a little bucket, which will bring up to the light of day some characteristic specimen, from those far depths, to be examined with a careful curiosity.

Our inquiry is necessarily very focused – we will be hauling to the surface those "characteristic specimens" relating chiefly to Keynes' investment precepts. Nevertheless, in carrying out these soundings, hopefully at least a flavor of Keynes' ample life will also be conveyed to the reader. To extend Strachey's metaphor, occasionally we will have cause to divert our gaze beyond the objects of our immediate scrutiny and toward the expansive, sometimes turbulent ocean that constituted the life of John Maynard Keynes.

1.

THE APOSTLE MAYNARD

THE WORLDLY PHILOSOPHER

> *Some surprise has been expressed about the large fortune left by Lord Keynes. Yet Lord Keynes was one of the few economists with the practical ability to make money.*
>
> —*Financial Times*, September 30, 1946

IN SEPTEMBER 1946, FIVE MONTHS after his death, the bequest of John Maynard Keynes was made public. His net assets totaled just under £480,000 – of which around £400,000 was in stocks and other securities, with the bulk of the remainder comprising his art collection and rare books – the equivalent of around $30 million in today's money. Although Keynes had secured a number of board positions at leading City institutions and had received considerable royalties from some of his better-selling books, general amazement greeted news of his fortune. He had, after all, spent most of the preceding six years as an unpaid Treasury adviser; his parents had outlived him and therefore provided no inheritance; and Keynes, a great arts patron, had funded many cultural ventures out of his own pocket.

As suggested in the salmon-pink pages of the *Financial Times*, it was indeed Keynes' skill in the art of moneymaking that contributed to the bulk of his riches. Keynes' facility with money was not just limited to his own account, however. King's College – Keynes' spiritual, intellectual, and sometimes physical home – was also a beneficiary of his financial acumen. In its obituary on Keynes, the *Manchester Guardian* reported that:

> As bursar of his own college in Cambridge ... he was conspicuously successful, and by bold and unorthodox methods he increased very greatly the value of its endowments.

Although little known to the wider world, in certain circles Keynes' investment expertise was prized. There are stories of other college bursars making the pilgrimage to King's College, where Keynes would lounge Buddha-like and regally impart investment wisdom to an eager audience. A colleague noted that "such was his influence in the City and his reputation abroad" that markets would move in response to his speeches delivered as Chairman of the National Mutual Life Assurance Society. He sat on the boards of numerous investment companies, from which he would, with the unwavering conviction of a papal decree, declaim his views on the stock market and government economic policy.

This aspect of Keynes – the shrewd investor, the canny player of financial markets – is rather unexpected in light of the man's early life and beliefs. Keynes was an aesthete, his first allegiance to philosophy and the art of living well. At school and university he displayed little interest in worldly matters, and for the remainder of his life exhibited an intensely ambivalent attitude to the pursuit of wealth. He believed in Francis Bacon's dictum that money makes a good servant but a bad master – in Keynes' formulation, money's merit lay solely in its ability to secure and maintain the conditions allowing one to "live wisely and agreeably and well." Like economics itself, money was a mere expedient, nothing other than "a means to the enjoyment and realities of life", and moneymaking little more than an "amusement."

Before proceeding to an examination of Keynes' investment activities and techniques, a brief survey of the early influences on the man's life is appropriate. For although Keynes did not take up speculation and investing with any particular ardor until his mid-thirties, the attitudes that shaped his views on moneymaking were largely formed in his early years.

ENTER THE HERO

> *I like the name suggested – John Maynard Keynes sounds like the substantial name of the solid hero of a sensible novel.*
>
> —Keynes' grandfather, June 6, 1883

In the late nineteenth century, Britain was still the world's most powerful nation – "workshop of the world" and boasting an empire on which, famously, the sun never set. Other than occasional episodes of colonial disobedience, it had been decades since Britannia had been obliged to flourish her spear at an enemy of any substance. Before the Crimean War of the mid-1850s the last general European conflict was the Battle of Waterloo in 1815, in which the United Kingdom and its allies finally ended Napoleon's quest for French glory. Compared with the horrors and madness of the succeeding century, the Victorian era was a remarkable oasis of peace.

Emboldened by Adam Smith's paradoxical doctrine that selfish private actions would be transmuted into public virtues, and later by Darwin's observations on natural selection and survival of the fittest, *fin de siècle* British society embraced free trade and a substantially laissez-faire government. The spirit of competition and endeavor pervaded Queen Victoria's nation. Notwithstanding attacks on the flanks by the likes of Oscar Wilde and George Bernard Shaw, Britons fervently believed in the virtues of duty, hard work, and thrift. The stiff upper lip would, just occasionally, quiver and curl into a slight smirk of satisfaction when the British contemplated the patent superiority of their race.

Into this world of security, prosperity, and solid bourgeois values came John Maynard Keynes. He was born in June 1883 in the university town of Cambridge, his father an economics fellow at the University and his mother one of its first female graduates. Maynard, as he was known to family and friends, was subsequently joined by two siblings who themselves would figure in English public life – Geoffrey, later an eminent surgeon and bibliographer, and husband to Charles Darwin's granddaughter; and Margaret, like her mother a prominent social reformer and destined to marry a Nobel Prize winner in medicine.

A PRIVILEGED BOY

Education: the inculcation of the incomprehensible into the indifferent by the incompetent.

—Keynes (attributed)

Appropriately for one of the first true offspring of Cambridge University – for it was only in the late 1870s that the ancient statutes preventing Cambridge dons from marrying were repealed – Keynes shone intellectually. After a precocious childhood, bolstered by a rigorous study regimen devised by his father, Keynes secured a scholarship to Eton College, school of choice for British royalty and the nation's elite. Once at Eton, Keynes maintained his academic ascendancy, winning over sixty prizes during his five years there. Unlike some other Old Etonians such as Eric Blair, better known to the reading public as George Orwell, he also prospered socially and was elected College prefect in his final year at school.

Even at Eton, an institution not generally known for the humility of its incumbents, Keynes displayed an inordinate degree of intellectual haughtiness. One schoolmaster remarked, "I should like in certain things to see him a little more dissatisfied, a little more ready to note the points in which he fails." Another observed that "[Keynes] gives one the idea of regarding himself a privileged boy with perhaps a little intellectual conceit." He was quick-witted and cutting – he wrote of one of Charles Darwin's sons that "his hands certainly looked as if he might be descended from an ape," and complained that one particular schoolmaster was "dull and soporiferous beyond words ... I shall not suffer from want of sleep this half." He embraced the prejudices of the upper middle class, holding in equal contempt the "absurd" aristocracy and the "boorish" lower classes – only the "intelligentsia," of which the Keynes family was a prime example, commanded his respect.

Like most other Establishment institutions of the time, Eton exhibited a snobby disregard for commercial matters. The school had long been the proving ground for young gentlemen of the Empire – the Duke of Wellington famously, if apocryphally, affirmed that the Battle of Waterloo was won on Eton's playing fields – and there was little room for the ungallant trade of the businessman in this sanctuary of old world values. The only hint of Keynes' subsequent career as an economist and investor was the schoolboy's obsessive preoccupation with lists and numbers – Keynes scrupulously recorded cricket scores, train times, hours worked, variations in his body temperature, and even "the comparative lengths of some long poems" during his time at Eton.

THE CAMBRIDGE IDYLL

> *The appropriate subjects of passionate contemplation and communion were a beloved person, beauty and truth, and one's prime objects in life were love, the creation and enjoyment of aesthetic experience and the pursuit of knowledge.*
>
> —Keynes on the Apostles, *My Early Beliefs*

On the back of a scholarship to King's College, Keynes returned to Cambridge in 1902 to study mathematics and classics. With customary chutzpah, he announced in his freshman year that "I've had a good look round the place and come to the conclusion that it's pretty inefficient." Although a gifted mathematician, he was by no means a prodigy, and in late 1905 placed twelfth of those receiving a First Class degree. While at university Keynes also found time to cultivate his social interests, and in his final undergraduate year became president of the Cambridge Union and president of the Liberal Club.

The most important influence on Keynes while at Cambridge was a secret society known to initiates as "the Apostles." This group recruited from the promising young men of Cambridge – E. M. Forster, Wittgenstein, and Bertrand Russell were fellow members – and its defining principles were best expressed in G. E. Moore's *Principia Ethica*, published during Keynes' first year at Cambridge. Moore's philosophy was profoundly non-materialistic and unworldly – Keynes once commented that, in comparison to the *Principia*, "the New Testament is a handbook for politicians." Moore, a Cambridge academic, believed that:

> By far the most valuable things, which we know or can imagine, are certain states of consciousness, which may be roughly described as the pleasures of human intercourse and the enjoyment of beautiful objects.

Many of the Apostles applied a very particular interpretation to Moore's endorsement of the pleasures of human intercourse. In the cloistered and covert world of the society, where aesthetic experience and intimate friendships were paramount, relations often transcended the merely platonic. Keynes reminisced many years later that "we repudiated entirely customary morals, conventions, and traditional wisdom ... [and] recognized no moral obligation on us, no inner sanction, to conform or to obey."

Standing aloof from the masses, the Apostles developed a superiority complex to match the belief that only they possessed the requisite sensitivity to truly appreciate the finer things in life. Keynes likened the group to "water-spiders, gracefully skimming, as light and reasonable as air, the surface of the stream without any contact at all with the eddies and currents underneath." Others, less charitably, dismissed the group as self-indulgent and ridiculous, twisting Moore's philosophy into "a metaphysical justification for doing what you like and what other people disapprove of."

AN INDIA MAN

Cecily, you will read your Political Economy in my absence. The chapter on the Fall of the Rupee you may omit. It is somewhat too sensational. Even these metallic problems have their melodramatic side.

—Oscar Wilde, *The Importance of Being Earnest*

Reality eventually intruded into Keynes' life and, after graduating in mathematics, the practical question of how to earn a living confronted him. He toyed with the idea of undertaking a second degree in economics, and for a while attended lectures given by Professor Alfred Marshall, a personal friend of the Keynes family and probably the world's most influential economist at the time. Despite Marshall's entreaties – "I trust your future career may be one in which you will not cease to be an economist," the Professor implored – Keynes eventually opted for a career as a government man. In August 1906 he sat for the nationwide Civil Service examination, where he placed second overall. Ironically, his worst mark was in economics, prompting Keynes to remark that "the examiners presumably knew less than I did."

Unable to secure his first choice of government department – the Treasury – Keynes became a cog in the machine of Empire, moving to London and joining the India Office as a junior clerk in October 1906.

In those days of the "gold standard" – the convention then prevailing in most Western nations, whereby a country's exchange rate was determined by its reserves of gold – India's rather less domesticated monetary system attracted considerable interest among theoretical economists, and may have been influential in Keynes' career choice. Despite the alleged allure of the maverick rupee, however, Keynes found the India Office singularly unexciting. Unedifying tasks such as arranging the shipment of ten stud bulls to Bombay, Keynes' first assignment, undoubtedly presented a rude contrast to the rarefied climes he had inhabited in Cambridge.

THE BLOOMSBURY REBELLION

> *We were out to construct something new; we were in the van of the builders of a new society which should be free, rational, civilized, pursuing truth and beauty. It was all tremendously exhilarating.*
>
> —Leonard Woolf on the Bloomsbury group

Offsetting the dullness of the Civil Service was the loose and fluctuating coterie of artists, writers, and philosophers who coalesced at the residence of Virginia Woolf and her siblings. Like the Apostles before them, the Bloomsbury group – named after the London district of garden squares and grand houses – reveled in confounding the traditional pieties and restraints of society. A herald of the counterculture movement later that century and the original bourgeois Bohemians, one "Bloomsberry" later recounted:

> We found ourselves living in the springtime of a conscious revolt against the social, political, religious, moral, intellectual, and artistic institutions, beliefs, and standards of our fathers and grandfathers.

The group's willingness to slough conventional modes of thought and behavior naturally extended to the more intimate domain of personal relationships. Bloomsbury affairs were notoriously labyrinthine and prickly – it was said that Bloomsberries "lived in squares but loved in triangles." Romantic intrigues, betrayals, and sniping provided a diversion from earnest discussions on art, ideas, and the meaning of life, and members of the group sometimes used their artistic gifts in the service of less than genteel verbal assaults. Virginia Woolf, in a fit of pique, once likened Keynes to "a gorged seal, double chin, ledge of red lip, little eyes, sensual, brutal, unimaginative," although this outburst could quite possibly have been in response to Keynes' gentle suggestion that she stick to nonfiction.

The more conservative elements of society regarded the Bloomsberries with open hostility. John Buchan, author of *The Thirty-Nine Steps* and a stalwart Victorian, dismissed them as:

> the usual round-up of rootless intellectuals ... terribly knowing and disillusioned and conscientiously indecent ... a smattering not so much of facts as of points of view ... They took nothing for granted except their own surpassing intelligence

Although indeed possessed of a stratospheric self-importance, the group's pretensions were not completely unfounded. They were outriders for new styles of thought and artistic expression, and – ironically for a medley of such unrestrained egos – were instrumental in shepherding other, greater, artists and thinkers before the public eye. Picasso, Freud, Proust, Cézanne, and Matisse, among others, entered the English-speaking world largely through the Bloomsbury portal.

THE UNCIVIL SERVANT

> *I work for a Government I despise for ends I think criminal.*
>
> —Keynes to Duncan Grant, December 15, 1917

Defeated by the tedium of the job, Keynes resigned from the India Office in June 1908 and returned to King's College, where he submitted a dissertation on probability – according to one newspaper, "a thesis on mathematics so advanced that it was said that only three people on earth could understand it." He was elected to a fellowship in March 1909 and, although having no formal qualifications in the subject, taught economics and finance at Cambridge. Keynes became a polished and popular teacher, with some lectures – particularly those relating to the stock exchange – drawing capacity crowds.

During this time at Cambridge Keynes began to ascend the ladder of academia and public life. In 1911 he was appointed editor of the *Economic Journal*, perhaps the world's leading professional economics periodical at the time. Less than two years later, his first book, *Indian Currency and Finance*, was published and Keynes became a member of the Royal Commission on Indian Finance – a prestigious appointment for someone not yet thirty years of age. Keynes' Cambridge idyll was shattered, however, in the balmy summer of 1914 when Queen Victoria's grandsons Willy and Georgie – Kaiser Wilhelm II of Germany and King George V of Britain – led their nations into the first great conflict of the new century.

The declaration of war in August 1914 drew Keynes back to the Civil Service, this time at Treasury where he advised on the financing of the British war effort. Keynes' Bloomsbury acquaintances, fiercely pacifist, objected to his new role. One challenged Keynes:

> What are you? Only an intelligence that they need in their extremity … A genie taken incautiously out of King's … by savages to serve them faithfully for their savage ends, and then – back you go in to the bottle.

Despite their high-minded criticism of his role as a hired gun in the "European blood feud," as Keynes labeled the Great War, the Bloomsberries were not averse to exploiting Keynes' increasing influence within the Establishment. He often appeared before tribunals as an advocate for those male members of the group seeking to avoid the draft. In a hearing for Lytton Strachey – delicate aesthete and Keynes' one-time paramour – the army prosecutor demanded to know what Strachey would do if a Hun attempted to rape his sister. Poker-faced, he replied in his peculiarly squeaky voice, "I should try and come between them."

Keynes was "absolutely and completely desolated" by the carnage of the war and the government's determination to pursue victory at any cost. Many of his university friends, including the celebrated poet and patriot Rupert Brooke, remained forever on the foreign fields where they fell. In a tragic ambush of the old world by the new, these sons of the upper classes were invariably ordained "officer material" and, honoring the traditions of ages past, obliged to march into battle at the head of their men – only to be met by the murderous steel storms of modern weaponry. Keynes' letters to his former classmates were sometimes returned to him unopened, the bleak epitaph "Killed" scrawled across them.

Frustrated and conflicted over his role as an intellectual mercenary for the war effort, Keynes' reputation for arrogance and condescension ripened. On a trip to the United States in 1917 he made a "terrible impression for his rudeness." The British Ambassador to the United States noted in his high camp style that:

> This morning we got a visit from [Keynes] … who was very Treasuriclarkacious and reduced Dicky to silentious rage and Malcolm to a high treble. He was really too offensive for words and I shall have to take measures. He is also a Don and the combination is not pleasing. He is also a young man of talent and I presume the rule for such nowadays is to show his immense superiority by crushing the contemptible insignificance of the unworthy outside.

Keynes was beginning to find his voice – the impudent junior rebuking his masters, the gadfly nipping at the flanks of a complacent Establishment, the double agent within the citadel, valuing truth above expediency.

A CARTHAGINIAN PEACE

> *Words ought to be a little wild, for they are the assault of thoughts upon the unthinking.*
>
> —Keynes, *National Self-Sufficiency*

Expected by most to last only a few months, it was four years before the war finally gave way to an armistice in November 1918. France, which lost a staggering 1.4 million men during the conflict, was determined to make Germany pay dearly for its perceived belligerence. Britain, which together with its dominions recorded close to a million men dead, was initially more conciliatory. The British Prime Minister, David Lloyd George, observed in March 1919 that the preservation of peace on the Continent would depend "upon there being no causes of exasperation constantly stirring up either the spirit of patriotism, of justice, or of fair play, to achieve redress." Accordingly, he advocated peace terms:

> dictated … in the spirit of judges sitting in a cause which does not personally engage their emotion or interests, and not in a spirit of savage vendetta, which is not satisfied without mutilation and the infliction of pain and humiliation.

Despite these lofty words, the Paris Peace Conference degenerated into an unseemly auction of the aggrieved, a contest among the victors as to which could carve the most from the husk of central Europe. In an effort to appease constituents at home and deliver on promises to "make Germany pay," the Allied leaders imposed a war guilt clause on Germany – an explicit statement that the German state and its confederates were solely responsible for the Great War – and also a reparations clause requiring Germany to "make compensation for all damage done to the civilian population of the Allied and Associated Powers and to their property."

Keynes, attached to the British delegation as an economic adviser, scorned the shortsightedness of the Allied leaders:

> The future life of Europe was not their concern; its means of livelihood was not their anxiety. Their preoccupations, good and bad alike, related to frontiers and nationalities, to the balance of power, to imperial aggrandizements, to the future enfeeblement of a strong and dangerous enemy, to revenge, and to the shifting by the victors of their unbearable financial burdens on to the shoulders of the defeated.

On his thirty-sixth birthday, June 5, 1919, and as the Treaty of Versailles was being finalized, Keynes resigned in protest at the "Carthaginian peace" to be imposed on the vanquished nations.

Freed from the constraints of the Civil Service, he produced in only a few months a withering critique of the Conference. *The Economic Consequences of the Peace*, published in December 1919, was a sensation – translated into eleven languages and selling over 100,000 copies in its first full year of publication. The book was celebrated as much for its bravura portraits of key Conference participants as for its political and economic arguments. Keynes depicted the American President Woodrow Wilson as a "blind and deaf Don Quixote" who "like Odysseus ... looked wiser when he was seated," and the French leader Georges Clemenceau as a xenophobe with "one illusion – France; and one disillusion – mankind." Warming to his theme, he parodied Lloyd George as "this goat-footed bard, this half-human visitor to our age from the hag-ridden magic and enchanted woods of Celtic antiquity." Cooler heads eventually persuaded

Keynes to withhold this last pen portrait from the published version of his book.

In a conclusion of frightening prescience, Keynes declared that the aggressive reparations terms would return to haunt the Continent:

> If we aim deliberately at the impoverishment of Central Europe, vengeance, I dare predict, will not limp. Nothing can then delay for very long that final civil war between the forces of reaction and the despairing convulsions of revolution, before which the horrors of the late German war will fade into nothing, and which will destroy, whoever is victor, the civilization and the progress of our generation.

DISESTABLISHED

> *The book in a certain sense was the turning point in Lord Keynes' career. Thereafter he was no longer a mere economist but a prophet and pamphleteer, a journalist and the author of a best seller.*
>
> —*The New York Times* on *The Economic Consequences of the Peace*

In a pattern that would be repeated over the rest of his life, Keynes' robust take-no-prisoners style polarized opinions. Many derided his perceived pro-German sympathies – some mockingly referring to him as "Herr Johann von Keynes," others suggesting he be awarded an Iron Cross – and he was cast on the outer by the government he had so effectively ridiculed. *The Economic Consequences of the Peace* marked Keynes' transformation from a mere government functionary operating on the periphery of diplomacy and academia to an influential and dissident public figure – he commented that, following publication of the book, "I woke up like Byron, famous and disreputable."

Notwithstanding his newfound notoriety, Keynes – jobless after resigning from Treasury – desperately needed another source of income to sustain the rather lavish lifestyle to which he and the Bloomsbury circle had become accustomed. Putting his money where his mouth was, Keynes decided to back the pessimistic views expressed in *Economic Consequences* by speculating heavily on the foreign exchange market, taking short positions on key Continental currencies and long positions on the U.S. dollar. Keynes believed he was ideally equipped to play the speculation game – having lectured on the subject at Cambridge, he knew something of finance and exchanges; his stint at Treasury had provided an insight into global realpolitik and the interplay of capital flows; and he had ready access to a pool of investors willing to back his trading activities.

Additionally, speculation offered the pleasing prospect of earning considerable amounts of money relatively painlessly. Like his contemporary Winston Churchill, much of Keynes' business was transacted while lounging in his bed. As one of his biographers noted:

> Some of this financial decision-making was carried out while he was still in bed in the morning; reports would come to him by phone from his brokers, and he would read the newspapers and make his decisions.

It is to this incarnation of Keynes – the aesthete, the outsider, the languid speculator – that we now turn.

2.

CITIZEN KEYNES

THE LAPSED APOSTLE

Yet I glory
More in the cunning purchase of my wealth
Than in the glad possession.

—Ben Jonson, *Volpone*

MAYNARD KEYNES WAS A PARADOXICAL figure – a Bohemian eventually embraced by the Establishment, an aesthete who prospered in the world of Mammon, the savior of capitalism with scant regard for the free enterprise system. In his opinions, too, Keynes was mercurial, embodying Emerson's dictum that a foolish consistency is the hobgoblin of little minds. He was notoriously contradictory and capricious – Churchill is said to have remarked that "whenever I ask England's six leading economists a question, I get seven answers – two from Mr. Keynes." David Lloyd George – still smarting from Keynes' hatchet job in *The Economic Consequences of the Peace* – complained that Keynes "dashed at conclusions with acrobatic ease. It made things no better that he rushed into opposite conclusions with the same agility."

Perhaps nowhere was Keynes' capacity for contradiction more evident than in his attitude to money and the pursuit of wealth. The righteous author who railed against the "rentier bourgeoisie" for subordinating "the arts of ... enjoyment" to compound interest in *Economic Consequences* considerably softened his invective only a couple of years later. In a 1921 speech to a new batch of Apostles, Keynes referred to a recently deceased member of the club who had forsaken academia for life in the business world – a man whose intellectual capacities, Keynes remarked acidly, "were much in excess of those usually associated with the love of money." Keynes ventured the opinion that the deceased's mercantile acts were perhaps more in the nature of "artistry, not of avarice," and he summoned the image of a curious hybrid, a type of poet-plutocrat, participating in "the stir and bustle of the world, pitting his wits, at a price, against all comers ... [and] exercising a variety of conjoined gifts." Moneymaking, Keynes suggested to the undergraduates, could be viewed as a great game, a kind of high-stakes chess where the nimble minded could cash in on their intellectual superiority.

Although ostensibly a valedictory to a former Apostle, there is little doubt that Keynes was attempting to justify his own move into the world of finance and speculation. One part of Keynes despised the pursuit of wealth. In a later paper he would invoke a glowing future where:

> The love of money as a possession ... will be recognized for what it is, a somewhat disgusting morbidity, one of those semi-criminal, semi-pathological propensities which one hands over with a shudder to the specialists in mental disease.

The more pragmatic side of Keynes accepted, however, the incontrovertible fact that money was, to use Dostoyevsky's phrase, "coined liberty" and that "the enjoyments and realities of life" were withheld from those of little means.

From these two competing insights arose a typically Keynesian compromise: Keynes would leap headlong into the world of finance, but the task of moneymaking would not consume him. It would remain an amusement, a means to an end, a way of supporting his more worthy ventures. And if he could win at the expense of those who professed an overweening love of money, then so much the better.

THE SPECULATION RACKET

> *[Speculation is] my diversion, to avoid the possibility of tedium in a country life.*
>
> —Keynes to his mother, September 3, 1919

Before 1919, Keynes had shown only fitful interest in the financial markets. His first recorded investment was in 1905, at twenty-two years of age, when he bought shares in an insurance company and later an engineering firm using his "special fund" of birthday money and cash from academic prizes. Clive Bell, a close acquaintance, hazarded a guess that Keynes' real interest in the markets was not sparked until early 1914:

> Maynard, who at Cambridge and in early London days had barely glanced at "Stock Exchange Dealings," grew so weary ... of reading the cricket-scores in *The Times* that, while drinking his morning tea, he took to studying prices instead.

Keynes' investments until 1919 were relatively sporadic, but his portfolio – principally in the form of ordinary shares – enjoyed a steady increase in value, and by the end of 1918 he owned securities worth £9,428, around $625,000 in today's money.

Keynes began speculating in earnest in August 1919, in between correcting drafts of *The Economic Consequences of the Peace*. His activities were focused on the currency markets, where exchange rates, shorn free from the bedrock of the pre-War gold standard, would often jag wildly. Keynes' strategy was simple – backing the views expressed in his book, he was bearish on certain Continental currencies and bullish on the U.S. dollar. This policy proved extremely successful, and in the space of five months Keynes realized profits of just over £6,000, the equivalent of around $375,000 today. Buoyed by this, Keynes wrote to his mother that:

> Money is a funny thing … As the fruit of a little extra knowledge and experience of a special kind, it simply (and undeservedly in any absolute sense) comes rolling in.

Keynes' initial triumph engendered a grander scheme. He teamed up with a former Treasury colleague, Oswald Falk, to form a syndicate to speculate on currency movements. "Foxy" Falk, a partner in the aptly named stockbroking firm Buckmaster and Moore, was, like Keynes, a charismatic figure of firm views. One City acquaintance recalled of Falk that he:

> would not look after any private client unless he was given *carte blanche* to do what he liked. The poor victim either made a killing in the market or was wiped out completely.

Although Keynes had predicted that his financial speculation "will shock father," the enterprise was enthusiastically supported by family and friends, and the sum of £30,000 was quickly raised.

Keynes and Falk embarked upon their trading scheme in January 1920. Due to a perceived lack of liquidity in the currency market, Falk withdrew from the syndicate shortly afterward, but Keynes persevered and had realized profits of £9,000 after the first three months of operations. However, in May the market turned against the syndicate and losses began to swell – by midyear Keynes noted that the partnership had witnessed the "slaughter of a large part of our holdings." Keynes was stoic – "It has been a beastly time, but I have kept fairly philosophical," he confided to Bloomsberry Vanessa Bell – and his parents also seemed to accept the losses with good grace. Keynes' mother mused that:

> It was perhaps necessary to throw something overboard to propitiate the Gods – if they are content with mere money, we will not grudge it to them.

Undaunted, Keynes remounted the horse that had thrown him. He liquidated securities from his personal stock portfolio, procured an advance payment for royalties due on sales of *Economic Consequences*, and inveigled a £5,000 loan from King Edward's private banker, Sir Ernest Cassel. In his letter to Cassel, Keynes, despite having "quite exhausted my resources," thought that the foreign exchange market offered "an unequalled opportunity for speculation" and anticipated that Cassel would be rewarded with "very substantial profits with very good probability if you are prepared to stand the racket for perhaps a couple of months." Keynes' optimism was justified – toward the end of 1920 he repaid Cassel, and by December 1922 he had cleared all his syndicate debts and boasted net assets of just over £21,000, around $1.5 million in today's money.

THE ECONOMIST AND THE SHOWGIRL

> *As for Loppi don't marry her. Flight to India may save you. However charming she may be, she'd be a very expensive wife & would give up dancing & is altogether I'm sure much to be preferred as a mistress.*
>
> —Vanessa Bell to Keynes, January 1, 1922

Keynes' career as a City man was not, however, confined to the tumult of the currency market. Befitting a son of the Establishment, he fulfilled his gentlemanly destiny and accepted board positions at a number of insurance and investment companies. Keynes' first directorship was secured in September 1919 at the National Mutual Life Assurance Society, and throughout the early 1920s he continued to collect board appointments at various London finance houses. Away from the City, Keynes was elected Second Bursar of King's College in late 1919 and succeeded to First Bursar, or chief treasurer of the College, five years later.

Keynes' détente with mainstream respectability continued in 1925 when, to the absolute disbelief of the Bloomsbury set, the confirmed bachelor married the Russian prima ballerina Lydia Lopokova. The union garnered international headlines, with Keynes – despite his fame following *The Economic Consequences of the Peace* – playing a distinctly second fiddle to his exotic bride. Lydia was something of a tabloid darling – not only had she danced for the Tsar as a child, performed vaudeville in New York with Al Jolson, and been a lover of the composer Stravinsky, but had commandeered London headlines in 1919 when she fled the Ballets Russes, allegedly to elope with a Russian general. On the day of their marriage, a press scrum jostled outside the St. Pancras registry office to document the celebrity wedding – the lanky and slightly stooped figure of Keynes, grave in a dark suit and looking uncharacteristically abashed, and the tiny Lydia, presenting herself to the battery of photographers with the practised ease of a professional.

Lydia's childlike enthusiasms and stumbling misadventures with the English language – "You must come and see Lady B's ovary; she says it's the largest in England!" she once exclaimed, having glimpsed an acquaintance's collection of caged birds – charmed Keynes and proved a welcome diversion from the cynical Bloomsberries. Notwithstanding Keynes' previous romantic predilections – and an unpromising start to the marriage when the gloomy Austrian philosopher Ludwig Wittgenstein gatecrashed the couple's honeymoon – "Pupsik" and "Maynarochka," as they labeled themselves in their many letters, would remain a devoted pair for the rest of their married life.

IN GOLD WE TRUST

In truth, the gold standard is already a barbarous relic.

—Keynes, *A Tract on Monetary Reform*

Paralleling Keynes' transformation from libertine to faithful husband was his move away from the hustle and commotion of the currency markets and toward the slightly more civilized milieu of the stock exchange. Keynes' drift from currency speculation was largely prompted by the decision of Winston Churchill, then Chancellor of the Exchequer, to restore sterling to the gold standard in 1925. Tethering the pound to a fixed benchmark radically reduced relative price movements – and hence a speculator's opportunity for profit – in the currency market. Keynes strenuously opposed this move, but not just because it robbed him of a livelihood.

He asserted in *The Economic Consequences of Mr. Churchill* – published in August 1925, the same month as his marriage to Lydia – that the Chancellor had been "deafened by the clamorous voices of conventional finance ... and ... gravely misled by his experts" who recommended that sterling be restored to its pre-War exchange rate against the U.S. dollar. These "experts," Keynes thought, were unwilling to countenance the possibility that the pound had effectively weakened in the decade or so since the start of the Great War. He argued that their insistence on maintaining a strong currency – partly motivated, one suspects, by a vague and misplaced sense of national pride – would price many British exports out of the market, leading to unemployment and a further weakening of an already fragile economy. Despite the vigor of his protests, Keynes' jeremiad passed largely unheeded. As he remarked forlornly in a letter to *The Times*, "To debate monetary reform with a City editor ... is like debating Darwinism with a bishop sixty years ago."

COMPOUND INTEREST MACHINES

> *Money is of a prolific generating Nature.*
> *Money can beget Money, and its Offspring can beget more*
> —Benjamin Franklin, *Advice to a Young Tradesman*

Rather serendipitously, at around the same time Britain was cajoled back on to the gold standard – and, in consequence, currency trading opportunities dwindled – Keynes came across an "interesting little book" on equities. Edgar Lawrence Smith's *Common Stocks as Long-Term Investments* analyzed the relative performance of American common stocks and bonds from 1866 to 1922. Smith's original hypothesis was that an investment in common stocks would outperform an investment in bonds in a period of inflation, but the converse would be true in times of falling prices. This was an eminently reasonable assumption: businesses can generally hedge against inflation by increasing their prices to offset costs, but bond coupons remain fixed even in an environment of consistently rising prices.

By the early 1920s, the role of stocks as an "inflationary shield" was more than a mere academic footnote. Many Continental European nations, destabilized by the ravages of the Great War and struggling to service reparations obligations, suffered mind-boggling inflation. The German government, to cite the most extreme example, printed money at such a rate that hyperinflation seized the country – a loaf of bread costing less than 200 marks in 1922 escalated to 200 *billion* marks by November 1923. In an inversion of the conventional consumer experience, shoppers entered a store with a trolley-full of cash and left with only a handful of items. In this environment, the value of bonds and bank deposits, which pay a fixed money amount regardless of any erosion in purchasing power, was destroyed.

Although the value of stocks as a hedge against inflation was readily understood by the mid-1920s, accepted wisdom also held tenaciously to the assumed flip side of this finding – that in deflationary periods, bonds should outperform stocks. The results of Smith's study on the relative merits of stocks and bonds were, however, quite unexpected. Smith found that, overwhelmingly, ordinary shares outperformed bonds not only in inflationary periods but also in times of falling prices.

Smith attributed this result to a number of factors, the most important of which was the "compound interest" effect inherent in ordinary shares. As Keynes summarized in a review of Smith's book:

> Well-managed industrial companies do not, as a rule, distribute to the shareholders the whole of their earned profits. In good years, if not in all years, they retain a part of their profits and put them back into the business. Thus *there is an element of compound interest* operating in favor of a sound industrial investment. Over a period of years, the real value of the property of a sound industrial is increasing at compound interest, quite apart from the dividends paid out to the shareholders. Thus ... an index of shares yields *more* in the long run than its initial apparent rate of interest.

Smith's simple but profound observation – that equities were, in effect, "compound interest machines," offering not just dividends but capital growth through reinvestment of undistributed earnings – was a key factor in kick-starting the "cult of the common stock" in the mid-1920s.

A DEVOTEE OF THE CULT

> *[Ordinary shares] represent the live large-scale business and investment world of today, and any investment institution which ignores or is not equipped for handling their shares is living in a backwater.*
>
> —Keynes, National Mutual annual meeting, January 25, 1928

Seduced by "the dizzy virtues of compound interest," Keynes became a lead evangelist of the cult of the common stock. He extolled the merits of equities in book reviews, at shareholder meetings, and in memoranda to his investment brethren. Notwithstanding Keynes' considerable powers of persuasion – and despite common stocks being anointed as a legitimate investment vehicle as a result of Smith's study – convincing investment company boards and college funds to invest in equities was no easy task. Most financial institutions at the time considered stocks – which paid a variable dividend dependent on the underlying company's profits – to be far riskier than the comforting predictability of bond yields and property rents. In the first quarter of the twentieth century at least, gentlemen most definitely preferred bonds.

Undeterred, and with the fervor of any new convert, Keynes unceasingly browbeat his colleagues and eventually prevailed. By as early as 1926 the proportion of National Mutual's funds invested in ordinary shares was over three times the average stock holding of other British life assurance societies. Similarly, and after sustained lobbying by Keynes, the investment remit of the King's College "Chest Fund" – an endowment fund over which Keynes enjoyed sole managerial discretion – was broadened from the traditional focus on property and fixed-yield securities to also include investments in shares. Keynes' campaign to widen the scope of the Chest Fund contended against not only the inherent conservatism of College custodians, but also hidebound rules proscribing particular investments. Indeed, one campus conspiracy theory at the time attributed Keynes' steadfast opposition to the appointment of a law don to King's to his fear that, under expert scrutiny, the Chest Fund would be found to be in breach of certain arcane university statutes forbidding investments in equities.

GOTHAM A-GO-GO

> *MAMMON, n: The god of the world's leading religion. The chief temple is in the holy city of New York.*
>
> —Ambrose Bierce, *The Devil's Dictionary*

Unfortunately for Keynes, the fledgling investment manager, British stocks were at the time an exceptionally unexciting investment prospect – after a fleeting boom in 1920, the United Kingdom settled into a long economic winter. The defeat of Germany and its allies proved a Pyrrhic victory, and the power shift from the Old World to the New had been hastened to its conclusion by the Great War. By the end of the fighting, Britain had lost around a quarter of its offshore assets – the bulk of these pawned to the United States in return for wartime supplies – and had ceded its position as the world's largest creditor to its former colony. Efforts to boost Britain's industrial production – which, even by 1925, was still considerably less than its pre-War level – were hampered by what Keynes derided as the "gold fetters" of the re-introduced gold standard. With around one in ten of the work force jobless during the 1920s, the British economy stalled, and for the remainder of the decade the stock market stagnated in sympathy.

In contrast to the situation in Britain, a "high tide of prosperity," as Keynes termed it, washed the shores of the United States. An already faltering international gold standard had obliged the Federal Reserve to lower American interest rates, and – partly fuelled by this cheap money – the richest society ever known to the world had embarked on what F. Scott Fitzgerald later described as "the most expensive orgy in history."

Seemingly defying gravity and the tenets of common sense, the Dow Jones index – that seismograph of investor confidence – traced an almost vertical ascent in the last years of the 1920s. Wall Street climbed more in the eighteen months to September 1929 than it had in the previous five years combined, and market darlings such as the Radio Corporation of America doubled and then doubled again over this period.

Although Keynes' attitude to America was ambivalent – he once commented that "I always regard a visit [to the United States] as in the nature of a serious illness to be followed by a convalescence" – his enthusiasm for Wall Street was sincere. Like so many others in benighted Europe, Keynes looked longingly across the Atlantic to the bright lights and palpable energy of New York. The advent of wire services made offshore investment practicable and a buoyant Wall Street became the natural destination for European speculative capital. Although Keynes' dollar exposure during the 1920s represented only a very small portion of his personal portfolio, some of his investment companies were heavily invested in American securities, and in consequence he became an avid observer of the New York exchange. And it was to be on the febrile and frenetic Wall Street of the late 1920s that Keynes would encounter the extremes of investor psychology and discern the true nature of the stock market.

3.

SNAP, OLD MAID, AND MUSICAL CHAIRS

NOTHING BUT BLUE SKY

> *All people are most credulous when they are most happy.*
>
> —Walter Bagehot, *Lombard Street*

PRESIDENT CALVIN COOLIDGE was not known for his verbosity. It was said by one hostess that he spoke so infrequently that every time he opened his mouth a moth flew out. Once, responding to a dinner guest's confession of a bet that she could get the President to say at least three words during the meal, he replied, "You lose." However, in December 1928, in one of his last addresses as President, "Silent Cal" was moved to a rare eloquence. He proudly boasted that:

> No Congress of the United States ever assembled, on surveying the state of the Union, has met with a more pleasing prospect than that which appears at the present time ... The country can regard the present with satisfaction and anticipate the future with optimism.

At the end of 1928, a certain smugness about the state of the American economy seemed justified. Uncle Sam had grown fat on the remains of a Europe still recovering, dazed and haltingly, from the Great War. America was the world's undisputed economic superpower, but paradoxically it had turned inward, shaken by its brief, bloody excursion to the Old World. Exploiting its newfound wealth, the country instead sought consolation in a massive binge of retail therapy. The techniques of mass production, honed during the war, were now applied to the civilian sphere, and radios, automobiles, and myriad domestic appliances spilled off America's assembly lines. A nation of consumers was created to absorb this productive capacity – advertising and easy credit persuaded Americans to abandon their puritan peccadillos and embrace materialism.

The Jazz Age was born – that curious mix of moneymaking and frivolity, parties and Prohibition. It was as if the whole country was animated by the relentless tempo of the production line. In this feverish environment of getting and spending, the stock market became a national obsession. As one British visitor noted in 1929:

> You could talk about Prohibition, or Hemingway, or air conditioning, or music, or horses, but in the end you had to talk about the stock market, and that was when the conversation became serious.

Bellhops and shoe-shine boys dispensed stock tips, punters bought shares on margin, brokers opened offices on ocean liners so transatlantic passengers could imbibe the bounty of Wall Street. Borne aloft on updrafts of investor euphoria, the Dow Jones index doubled in only a couple of years.

Some commentators – noting a global system unbalanced by wartime debts and a domestic economy giddy on easy money – shook their heads and predicted an almighty financial hangover to follow the riotous Roaring Twenties. These Cassandras were, however, largely ignored. Wall Street pundits cited the improving effects of Prohibition on workers' productivity and the steadying influence of the Federal Reserve, among other factors, to support their contention that stock prices were fundamentally sound. Perhaps the most potent rejoinder to the doomsayers, however, was an explanation appealing to that most American of traits – faith in the democratic process. The argument was best summarized by Professor Joseph Stagg Lawrence of Princeton University who, late in the summer of 1929, posed the following rhetorical challenge:

> the consensus of judgment of the millions whose valuations function on that admirable market, the Stock Exchange, is that stocks are not at present prices over-valued. Where is that group of men with the all-embracing wisdom which will entitle them to veto the judgment of this intelligent multitude?

THE COLLECTIVE MIND

> *If everyone is thinking alike then somebody isn't thinking.*
>
> —General George S. Patton (attributed)

Professor Lawrence's reverence for the "intelligent multitude" anticipated the dogma later to be known as the "efficient markets hypothesis." This theory states that the stock exchange – meeting house, in Professor Lawrence's words, of "the consensus of judgment of the millions" – incorporates all public information which could possibly affect a stock's price, drawing on that sprawling resource, the investing public. Eugene Fama, the patriarch of the efficient markets theory explains the hypothesis in the following terms:

> In an efficient market, competition among the many intelligent participants leads to a situation where, at any point in time,

> actual prices of individual securities already reflect the effects of information based both on events that have already occurred and on events which, as of now, the market expects to take place in the future.

In defense of Professors Lawrence and Fama, there is considerable empirical evidence supporting the notion of the "intelligent multitude" – the idea that a group of decision makers can be greater than the sum of its parts. Prosaically, we have the so-called "*Who Wants to Be a Millionaire* phenomenon," where studio audiences give the correct answer around 90 percent of the time, significantly outperforming the nominated experts. Other examples – predicting election results, or setting the odds at horse races, or even guessing the number of jellybeans in a jar – all confirm that a group can be much smarter than most of its constituents. In the right environment, the unique opinions, knowledge, and perspectives of each component member of the group are brought to bear on the decision-making process, and from the rough and tumble of competing opinions emerges the polished stone of precision.

Intelligent group behavior, however, only flourishes where there is independence and diversity of opinion. As James Surowiecki explains in *The Wisdom of Crowds*:

> Independence is important to intelligent decision making for two reasons. First, it keeps the mistakes that people make from becoming correlated. Errors in individual judgment won't wreck the group's collective judgment as long as these errors aren't systematically pointing in the same direction ... Second, independent individuals are more likely to have new information rather than the same old data everyone is already familiar with.

Paradoxically, group intelligence will only manifest when participants act as if they are *not* part of a group.

THE PRICE IS RIGHT

> *The god of the cannibals will be a cannibal, of the crusaders a crusader, and of the merchants a merchant.*
>
> —Ralph Waldo Emerson, *The Conduct of Life*

The intelligent multitude thesis works best where the group draws on diverse knowledge sets, can make individual judgments independently, and has a mechanism for assimilating these judgments into a collective prediction or decision. The internet – an agglomeration of informed, atomistic individuals largely unconstrained by real-world complications, and the closest thing we have to the classical economic ideal of a "perfect market" – perhaps best illustrates the power of group intelligence. Google, for example, harnesses the decisions of millions of internet users to identify web pages most relevant to particular search criteria. Through the operation of abstruse algorithms, links from one web page to another are interpreted as a "vote" for that page, with these votes weighted so that the most visited pages are accorded greater influence than more obscure sites. Google – a meritocracy of millions of individuals' choices – generates an uncannily effective search tool from the distilled wisdom of the crowd.

In a similar manner, stock exchanges absorb the myriad views of thousands of individuals, all of whom may "vote" by electing to buy or sell their securities. In theory, the stock market should be a highly effective forum for the exercise of collective intelligence: it incorporates the decisions of many independent actors, each motivated by the opportunity of financial reward, and aggregates these judgments rapidly and transparently. Stockholders "voting" on the price of a security will bring their diverse perspectives to the process – including alternative information sources, differing time horizons, and contrasting investment styles. Efficient markets proponents argue that this arena of robustly competing opinions produces stock prices that embody, and appropriately weight, *all* publicly known information about a particular stock.

A corollary of the efficient markets hypothesis is that it is futile to try to beat the market. As Nobel laureate Paul Samuelson explains, the efficient markets theory teaches that there are no undiscovered bargains or overpriced time bombs lurking on the exchanges:

> If intelligent people are constantly shopping around for good value, selling those stocks they think will turn out to be overvalued and buying those they expect are now undervalued, the result of this action by intelligent investors will be to have existing stock prices already have discounted in them an allowance for their future prospects. Hence, to the passive investor, who does not himself search out undervalued and overvalued situations, there will be presented a pattern of stock prices that makes one stock about as good or bad a buy as another. To that passive investor, chance alone would be as good a method of selection as anything else.

Efficient markets fundamentalists deem the market – like God or his representative on earth – to be omniscient and infallible. Better for the individual to submit to this all-knowing entity, they argue, than waste his or her time trying to best it.

THE PIKE IN THE CARP-POND

> *As in the case of the bow and the lyre, there is harmony in the tension of opposites.*
>
> —Heraclitus

Despite the best efforts of orthodox dogma – which, at its simplest, assumes that all economic actors are members of that elevated species, the ultrarational, perfectly knowledgeable *homo economicus* – it is an incontrovertible fact that some individuals fall far short of the exacting standards of theory. In any stock market there will always be a proportion of participants willing to slipstream behind other investors, relying perhaps on the efficient markets theory to absolve them of the need to apply their own analysis. A market which counts the irrational, the uninformed, or the just plain lazy among its number can still, however, be efficient – provided there are enough sophisticated investors to rein in pricing anomalies caused by the less astute.

A Treasury official once recalled of Keynes that he "accepted a description of his functions as those of the pike put into the Roman carp-ponds to chase the carp around and keep them from getting lousy." Within the Civil Service, Keynes saw himself as a sort of devil's advocate, spurring his colleagues into action and attacking any perceived complacency. The efficient markets theory assumes a similar dynamic. Although there may indeed be slow-witted and inattentive investors in the market, the theory affirms that aberrations caused by their shortcomings will be exploited by their more sophisticated and nimble counterparts. Apparently underpriced stocks will be bid up, and overpriced stocks sold down, by the more efficient predators, maintaining the soundness of the market.

The efficient markets theory does not, therefore, demand that all market participants be the finely calibrated calculating machines of classical theory – merely that sufficient numbers of discerning investors exist so as to countervail the actions of the less sophisticated. In other words, there must be enough investors in any particular market who – disregarding the implications of the efficient markets theory – believe that there *are* in fact bargains to be had. It is these discriminating investors who ensure that markets remain efficient – they are the ever-vigilant pike, securing the overall health of the pond. The efficient markets theory, then, is like a perverse fairytale – one that comes true only if enough people do *not* believe in it.

SAFETY IN NUMBERS

One dog barks at something, and a hundred bark at the bark.

—Chinese proverb

Unfortunately for efficient markets proponents, individuals often cast aside their independence and instead seek the comfort of the crowd. Man, after all, is a social animal and, where possible, will rely on cues from his fellow creatures. The tendency to accede to the crowd may well be hard-wired: the caveman who, on seeing a torrent of people rushing past him, their faces contorted in a rictus of fear, declines to join the stampede is unlikely to have passed his genes on to posterity. Running with the mob is a primal response, particularly in times of panic or uncertainty, but even in more settled circumstances an individual will often seek the imprimatur of the majority.

"Social proof" – the belief that if a large number of people behave in a particular manner there must be a good reason for doing so – is a well-established psychological phenomenon. In the Asch conformity experiments of the 1950s, for example, a group of students was asked to judge the relative lengths of several lines. The catch was that all but one of the students were "insiders" instructed to give answers that were clearly incorrect. Despite obvious discomfort with their responses, around a third of the test subjects conformed to the erroneous view – they believed that the majority could simply not be wrong.

In circumstances such as these, the wisdom of the crowd degenerates into "groupthink" – a situation where each member of a group complies with the perceived consensus. Stock markets are particularly prone to this follow-the-crowd tendency. The bandwagon most conspicuously traverses the uncharted promised land of "new economy" industries – railways in the 1840s, radio in the 1920s, transistors in 1960s – where a technology is commercially unproven or not readily understood by the bulk of the investing public, and investors take their prompts from those seemingly in the know. The twentieth century's final speculative craze – the dot-com debacle of the 1990s – sported the holy trinity of bubble factors: an emerging technology, new commercial opportunities, and the means for groupthink to propagate itself in chat rooms where like-minded individuals could pontificate without fear of contradiction. Like some sinister self-replicating virus, fostering the conditions of its own flourishing, the internet bubble fed off the internet itself as day traders bid up "new economy" stock to unsustainable levels.

NIETZSCHE MARKET

> *When a hundred men stand together, each of them loses his mind and gets another one.*
>
> —Friedrich Nietzsche (attributed)

There is also, as Keynes observed, "a peculiar zest in making money quickly." Emulation and envy are powerful stimulants, and the desire to keep up with the Joneses often fuels herd behavior. The economist Charles Kindleberger wryly noted that "there is nothing so disturbing to one's well-being and judgment as to see a friend get rich," and the prospect of easy money on the stock exchange inevitably encourages others to venture their hand. Indeed, during booms the more cautious among the investment community are often castigated for their lack of entrepreneurial zeal. One observer of the "vortex of speculation" that gripped English railway stocks in the 1840s commented that:

> The few quiet men who remained uninfluenced by the speculation of the time were, in not a few cases, even reproached for doing injustice to their families, by declining to help themselves from the stores of wealth that were poured out on all sides.

Perhaps the most compelling explanation for the stock market's susceptibility to "informational cascades," however, is that, in some circumstances, herd behavior can appear to be a rational strategy – in the short term at least. A trend of rising stock prices will encourage others to purchase equities, which, in turn, reinforces the upward price trend. The economist John Kenneth Galbraith outlined the mechanics of these "positive feedback loops" in his book *A Short History of Financial Euphoria*:

> Some artifact or some development, seemingly new and desirable ... captures the financial mind ... The price of the object of speculation goes up ... This increase and the prospect attract new buyers; the new buyers assure a further increase. Yet more are attracted; yet more buy; the increase continues. The speculation building on itself provides its own momentum.

With magnificent circularity, rising prices lead to rising prices. Stock market players no longer apply their own judgment in valuing a particular stock, but rather look to trends in the market as their trading guide.

MOB RULE (SOMETIMES)

> *They called me mad, and I called them mad, and damn them, they outvoted me.*
>
> —Nathaniel Lee, Restoration playwright and Bedlam inmate

Financial exchanges, then, are particularly predisposed to "informational cascades" – episodes where the polarity of the market changes, and speculators predominate over more reasoned elements. The market reaches a pivot point where the intelligent multitude mutates into the unreasoning rabble, or, to use Keynes' metaphor, the schooling carp overwhelm the predatory pike. When the "smart money" is swamped by those scrambling aboard the bandwagon, the group is no longer intelligent and the market forfeits any claim to efficiency.

To paraphrase Oscar Wilde, a speculator is a man who knows the price of everything and the value of nothing. The speculator's concern is not to independently assess the value of a particular stock, but rather to divine the future movement of the market in an attempt to on-sell the stockholding at a profit. Keynes captured the mindset of the speculator perfectly:

> most of these persons are, in fact, largely concerned, not with making superior long-term forecasts of the probable yield of an investment over its whole life, but with foreseeing changes in the conventional basis of valuation a short time ahead of the general public. They are concerned, not with what an investment is really worth to a man who buys it "for keeps," but with what the market will value it at, under the influence of mass psychology, three months or a year hence.

It is the "greater fool" trading strategy – where, as Keynes noted, the speculators' objective is "to outwit the crowd, and to pass the bad, or depreciating, half-crown to the other fellow."

PASS THE PARCEL

> *In skating over thin ice, our safety is in our speed.*
>
> —Ralph Waldo Emerson, *Prudence*

Speculators walk a tightrope between staying in the market long enough to optimize trading gains, but not so long that the individual is caught in a bearish lurch downward. Keynes likened trading on a speculation-driven exchange to:

> a game of Snap, of Old Maid, of Musical Chairs – a pastime in which he is victor who says *Snap* neither too soon nor too late, who passed the Old Maid to his neighbor before the game is over, who secures a chair for himself when the music stops. These games can be played with zest and enjoyment, though all the players know that it is the Old Maid which is circulating, or that when the music stops some of the players will find themselves unseated.

The key task for the speculator is, therefore, to correctly *time* the purchase and sale of securities. Based on this belief, Keynes, in the early part of his investment career, thought that success on the stock market required little more than anticipating the anticipations of others. The rationale behind this strategy was set out in *A Treatise on Money*, written in the late 1920s:

> it may often profit the wisest [stock market player] to anticipate mob psychology rather than the real trend of events, and to ape unreason proleptically [i.e. in anticipation] … Thus, so long as the crowd can be relied on to act in a certain way, even if it be misguided, it will be to the advantage of the better-informed professional to act in the same way – a short period ahead.

Keynes' principal stock market trading strategy in the 1920s – which he christened "credit cycle investing" – faithfully reflected the market- timing approach of the typical speculator. Credit cycling was an application of the oldest stock market maxim in the book: buy low and sell high. As Keynes explained many years later, credit cycling in respect of common stocks "means in practice selling market leaders on a falling market and buying them on a rising one." It was a "top-down" approach to stock market investment, involving "a general systematic movement out of and into ordinary shares as a whole at different phases of the trade cycle." This approach – sometimes dignified with the slightly more scientific-sounding appellations of "momentum investing" or "anticipatory trading" – relies on the speculator's ability to apprehend turns in the market and time trades accordingly. For the "credit cycler," price momentum is the fundamental trading driver, rather than any assessment of the inherent value of a stock relative to its price.

An investment approach requiring the individual to anticipate something as fluid and capricious as "mob psychology" is, as Keynes would later discover, no easy undertaking. He compared the task to:

> those newspaper competitions in which the competitors have to pick out the six prettiest faces from a hundred photographs, the prize being awarded to the competitor whose choice most nearly corresponds to the average preferences of the competitors as a whole; so that each competitor has to pick, not those faces which he himself finds prettiest, but those which he thinks likeliest to catch the fancy of the other competitors, all of whom are looking at the problem from the same point of view. It is not a case of choosing those which, to the best of one's judgment, are really the prettiest, nor even those which average opinion genuinely thinks the prettiest. We have reached the third degree where we devote our intelligences to anticipating what average opinion expects the average opinion to be. And there are some, I believe, who practice the fourth, fifth and higher degrees.

Momentum investors operate in an Alice in Wonderland world of second-guesses – a crazy, reflexive hall of mirrors where individuals attempt to fathom "what average opinion expects the average opinion to be."

RUNNING OF THE BULLS

> *When stock prices are rising, it's called "momentum investing"; when they are falling, it's called "panic."*
>
> —Paul Krugman, *The New York Times*

Drawing on vast reserves of confidence and self-regard, Keynes convinced himself that he possessed the requisite foresight, skill, and agility to navigate the shifting shoals of market sentiment. Twenty years earlier, he had boasted to his undergraduate friend Lytton Strachey that:

> I want to manage a railway or organize a Trust, or at least swindle the investing public. It is so easy and fascinating to master the principles of these things.

Now, at last, Keynes had his opportunity to exploit the mob – to profit from the "gulls" and prove his intellectual superiority. He would, he assumed, successfully ride the cycle – dexterously picking market peaks and bottoms, second-guessing the enthusiasms and fears of the mass of individuals known in the abstract as "the market."

Keynes' unshakeable confidence in his own ability was a trait shared by many in those heady days of the late 1920s. Wall Street was firmly in the grip of a wave of investor euphoria, and while the stock exchange boomed, momentum investing was a game in which almost everyone could be a winner – as the old Wall Street saw reminds us, a rising tide lifts all boats. Although some naysayers liquidated their stockholdings in the summer of 1929, most others – reluctant to be the first to leave the party – maintained their portfolios, anticipating even greater profits in the future.

Charles Mitchell, Chairman of the National City Bank of New York and a noted market bull, typified the exuberant optimism of the time. He asserted in September 1929 that the market was "like a weather-vane pointing into a gale of prosperity." Unfortunately for Keynes and millions of others, Mitchell's meteorological metaphor was only half-right. Rather than a gale of prosperity, a perfect storm of financial destruction was bearing down on Wall Street.

4.

THE RECKONING

THE MUSIC STOPS

Booms go boom.

—Fred Schwed, *Where Are The Customers' Yachts?*

BY THE LATE 1920S, IRVING FISHER was America's most famous economist and financial pundit – a man who, like Keynes, achieved distinction in both academia and business. A professor of economics at Yale University, Fisher became a multimillionaire after his Index Visible Company, producer of an early version of the Rolodex, merged with Rand in 1925, with Fisher becoming a major shareholder in the new entity. In his unique position as theoretician, entrepreneur, and market player, Fisher was a shaman of the stock market, called upon at regular intervals to read the auguries of Wall Street – especially when the great god Market seemed restive and disobliging.

Fisher was Wall Street's Pollyanna, always ready to offer a reassuring comment or upbeat prognostication to the investing congregation. His great friend, but professional nemesis, was the securities analyst Roger Babson, dubbed "the Prophet of Loss" by New York newspapers.

Babson had presaged a stock market correction since 1926, but, like his fellow unbelievers, had been dismissed as little more than a "sand-bagger of American prosperity" by most market watchers. However, on September 5, 1929 – just two days after the Dow Jones Industrial Average had recorded an all-time high of 381.2 points – Babson's apprehensions finally found an audience. In a speech to group of businessmen, he warned:

> Sooner or later a crash is coming, and it may be terrific ... factories will shut down ... men will be thrown out of work ... the vicious circle will get in full swing and the result will be a serious business depression.

Wall Street fell around 3 percent that day, and the "Babson break" marked the beginning of six weeks of erratic trading.

Fisher, unsurprisingly, disputed Babson's dark and destabilizing predictions. In mid-October 1929, less than a fortnight before the Great Crash, the Professor stated, "Stock prices have reached what looks like a permanently high plateau ... I expect to see the stock market a good deal higher ... within a few months." His effort to quell the bears was, however, unsuccessful. On the morning of October 24, 1929 – "Black Thursday," as it later became known – the Wall Street bubble was pricked. Panic selling gripped the exchange in the morning, the financial hemorrhaging staunched only when a cabal of influential bankers ostentatiously stepped on to the trading floor, brandishing a pocketful of buy orders.

The intervention assuaged skittish investors, but only temporarily. Although the weekend break provided a respite from the gyrations of Wall Street, distance from the market also afforded a disturbingly grim vista to spooked shareholders. "Black Monday," October 28, was a financial bloodbath. The Dow Jones index fell by around 13 percent, and in some cases only a lack of buyers arrested the precipitate fall in stock prices. The following day – maintaining the swarthy theme, "Black

Tuesday" – witnessed another calamitous decline, this time by a further 12 percent. In that last week of October, stock ticker machines – overwhelmed by the unprecedented trading volume and disgorging tape long after the market had closed – tapped out a staccato requiem for the Great Bull Market of the 1920s.

NIGHTMARE ON WALL STREET

> *Some of the people I knew lost millions. I was luckier. All I lost was two hundred and forty thousand dollars ... I would have lost more but that was all the money I had.*
>
> —Groucho Marx, *Groucho and Me*

Irving Fisher, that unconquerable optimist, naturally imparted a sanguine spin to the October meltdown. He attributed the severe decline in the Dow Jones index to a "shaking out of the lunatic fringe" and in November 1929 volunteered the opinion that "the end of the decline of the Stock Market will probably not be long, only a few more days at most." In early 1930 he again tried to convince the market – and, in light of his massive exposure, perhaps himself – that "for the immediate future at least, the outlook [for stocks] is bright." Many others shared Fisher's dogged optimism – even Wall Street's archrealist, the financier Bernard Baruch, felt confident enough by mid-November to cable Winston Churchill with the unequivocal message that the "financial storm [has] definitely passed."

For a while, it looked as if the black days of late 1929 had indeed been nothing more than a pit stop on the road to prosperity. Wall Street was unusually volatile in the wake of the October tempest, but the overall trend was positive – by April 1930 the Dow Jones index was almost 30 percent above the depths plumbed six months earlier. But these brief flares of confidence turned out to be no more than "suckers' rallies," the last instinctive convulsions of a dying market. Wall Street resumed its descent in mid-1930, and by 1932 the Dow Jones Industrial Average stood at a miserable 41.2 points, a drop of almost 90 percent from its September 1929 peak. It would be a quarter of a century before the Dow Jones again reached the heights scaled during the Roaring Twenties.

Irving Fisher, like myriad other speculators and investors, was wiped out. He and his immediate family had borrowed money to buy additional Rand shares at the bull market's pinnacle, and his son later estimated Fisher's loss at around $10 million, well over $100 million in present-day terms. Fisher's insolvency obliged Yale University to buy his house and rent it back to him, with Fisher often unable to pay his new landlord. He came to the attention of the IRS for non-payment of tax, and was forced to borrow money from his wealthy sister-in-law. As a neoclassical economist whose professional interest was the study of rational markets, he was, for the remainder of his life, the butt of never-ending jokes for his naïve faith in ever-ascending stock prices.

PROPHET WARNING

> *Wall Street did have a go yesterday. Did you read about it? The biggest crash ever recorded ... I have been in a thoroughly financial and disgusting state of mind all day.*
>
> —Keynes to Lydia, October 25, 1929

In contrast to his American confrere, Keynes had substantially reduced his exposure to the stock market prior to the Great Crash of 1929. This move was not, however, attributable to any superior foresight on Keynes' account. Rather, his "terrifying adventures" on the speculative markets – this time, the commodities market – had once again brought him undone. In 1928, after several years of profitable trading, Keynes' positions in the rubber, corn, cotton, and tin markets turned against him, and he was obliged to liquidate the bulk of his equities to cover these losses.

The stock exchange upheavals of late 1929 then exacted a heavy toll on what little remained of Keynes' stock portfolio: his main holding – the Austin Motor Car Company – lost over three-quarters of its value in the final two years of the 1920s. In aggregate, Keynes' net worth declined by more than 80 percent over this period – from £44 000 at the start of 1928 to less than £8,000 two years later – and, for the second time in his life, he found himself poised on the precipice of financial ruin.

Despite the assault on his wealth, Keynes initially shared Fisher's confidence that the events of late 1929 were mere "corrections." He assured readers of the *New York Evening Post* the day after Black Thursday that "commodity prices will recover and farmers will find themselves in better shape." However, by as early as November 1929 his view on the situation had darkened considerably. Keynes thought that a major economic downturn was imminent and recommended to his fellow directors that the Independent Investment Company, which was heavily invested in Wall Street, sell its securities and repay outstanding debts. By May 1930, Keynes was broadcasting his bleak message to a much wider audience:

> The fact is – a fact not yet recognized by the great public – that we are now in the depths of a very severe international slump, a slump which will take its place in history amongst the most acute ever experienced. It will require not merely passive movements of bank rates to lift us out of a depression of this order, but a very active and determined policy.

THE CANARY IN THE COAL MINE

> *It was borrowed time anyhow – the whole upper tenth of a nation living with the insouciance of grand dukes and the casualness of chorus girls.*
>
> —F. Scott Fitzgerald, *Echoes of the Jazz Age*

The events of October 1929 were in fact an early symptom – rather than the cause – of a far more malignant malady. The Wall Street sideshow had diverted attention away from unsustainable imbalances within the wider community – as the economic historian Robert Heilbroner noted, just prior to the Crash, "some twenty-four thousand families at the apex of the social pyramid received a stream of income three times as large as six million families squashed at the bottom." Credit had largely been channeled away from the real economy and into financial speculation and conspicuous consumption, and while easy money stoked the speculative inferno of the late 1920s, farmers and other primary producers struggled with poor prices and mounting debts.

The gilded mansion of American prosperity proved to be top-heavy and teetering, perched precariously on the sandy foundations of installment credit and margin loans. The tremors on Wall Street had finally brought down this house of cards. There were foreclosures, runs on banks, and, ultimately, masses of workers laid off. By 1933, a quarter of the United States work force was unemployed, industrial production was only half that of 1929, and real income per capita had fallen to levels not seen since the start of the century. Over 5,000 banks had gone to the wall and "Hoovervilles" – shanty towns of the dispossessed – scarred the country, like open sores on the body politic.

The Wall Street contagion quickly spread beyond American frontiers, the web of obligations arising from the Versailles settlement entangling nations and frustrating their best efforts to quarantine the growing financial pandemic. Worse still, in a Canute-like effort to hold back the deadening tide, Western governments sought refuge behind ever-higher trade barriers. In dismantling the structure of free trade, the developed world was slowly dismembering its golden goose – this protectionist race to the bottom halved the volume of international trade in the four years following the Crash. Deprived of the oxygen of commerce, the world swooned into a state of near paralysis.

CARPE DIEM

> *But this* long run *is a misleading guide to current affairs.* In the long run *we are all dead. Economists set themselves too easy, too useless a task if in tempestuous seasons they can only tell us that when the storm is long past the ocean is flat again.*
>
> —Keynes, *A Tract on Monetary Reform*

With increasing urgency, Keynes exhorted governments to act decisively to wrest the Western world from "the bog" into which it had sunk – "Activity and boldness and enterprise," he told a radio audience in early 1931, "must be the cure." His pleas were, however, largely ignored by the practitioners of sound finance. Conventional wisdom counseled a policy of "liquidationism" – letting the hard times "purge the rottenness out of the system," in the words of Andrew Mellon, then the United States Secretary of the Treasury. These high priests of orthodox finance argued that the slump was no more than a rather spectacular manifestation of the "business cycle" which coursed through all developed economies, and that, ultimately, the Western world would right itself and full employment be restored.

Business cycles had long been viewed as an inevitable feature of advanced societies. The first recorded economic forecast had, after all, been Joseph's prediction of seven years of plenty followed by seven years of famine in Pharaonic Egypt, and Keynes himself had been born in the middle of what had been termed "the Great Depression" until it was trumped by the far more serious calamity of the 1930s. Indeed, downturns were welcomed by many as a type of Darwinian spring cleaning, in which underperforming enterprises are winnowed from the commercial world. Certain "austere and puritanical souls," Keynes would later remark, even viewed slumps as a kind of divine retribution by the market, as:

> an inevitable and a desirable nemesis on so much overexpansion, as they call it; a nemesis on man's speculative spirit. It would, they feel, be a victory for the mammon of unrighteousness if so much prosperity was not subsequently balanced by universal bankruptcy.

Implicit in the idea of business *cycles*, however, is the notion that – as surely as spring follows winter – the economy will at some stage revert to its previous prosperity. Classical economics, as Keynes summarized, presumed that:

> the existing economic system is, in the long run, a self-adjusting system, though with creaks and groans and jerks, and interrupted by time lags, outside interference and mistakes.

Despite the ferocity of the Great Depression, orthodoxy's faith in the efficacy of markets remained largely intact, seemingly unperturbed by the millions of unemployed, the destitution of families, and the unraveling of nations. Keynes abhorred the easy complacency of classical hardliners, and their serene assurances to the masses that society would *eventually* emerge from the Great Slump. In a stark rejoinder to the liquidationists selling their scorched earth policies, he reminded them that "in the long run we are all dead." In the time of its greatest crisis, capitalism simply did not have the luxury of waiting for the economy to heal itself.

THE CROAKINGS OF A CASSANDRA

> *During the past 12 years I have had very little influence, if any, on policy. But in the role of Cassandra, I have had considerable success as a prophet.*
>
> —Keynes, speech to Members of Parliament, September 16, 1931

As the 1930s stuttered on, there was scant evidence that the developed world was returning to health. Economies wallowed, unemployment levels remained stubbornly persistent, rumblings of discontent grew bolder, and citizens became restive. In 1932 U.S. Army units – commanded by Douglas MacArthur and George Patton, and assisted by Dwight Eisenhower in his first taste of armed conflict – brutally cleared with bayonets and tanks and teargas the makeshift camps of thousands of war veterans who had marched on the Capitol demanding government aid. That same year in Britain – where official unemployment levels averaged 20 percent nationally, and up to 70 percent in some regions – Sir Oswald Mosley, a former Government minister, seeded the British Union of Fascists in the fertile soil of discontent and despair. And on Continental Europe, the Great Depression acted as a kind of giant centrifuge – hurling men and women away from the political center, toward the extremes of socialism and fascism.

Keynes' gravest forebodings had come to pass. He had warned that the harsh tribute extracted from the Central Powers under that "damnable and disastrous document," the Versailles Treaty, would create insoluble international tensions. Later, he predicted that a return to the gold standard at pre-War exchange rates would severely distort trade and capital flows. And, now, as the world lurched even further into the morass, he despaired at the "beggar-thy-neighbor" policies of increasingly protectionist governments, remarking that:

> The modern capitalist is a fair-weather sailor. As soon as a storm rises, he abandons the duties of navigation and even sinks the boats which might carry him to safety by his haste to push his neighbor off and himself in.

Civilization, Keynes realized, rested on "a thin and precarious crust." He believed that the standard nostrum of classical theory – letting "matters take their natural course" – was inadequate and, moreover, misguided. Keynes, with the dubious advantage of already having lived through a decade-long recession in Britain, realized that the Great Depression was more than a merely cyclical phenomenon, and that there were fundamental structural factors which prevented the world from hauling itself out of the quagmire. He had previously used newspaper articles, pamphlets, open letters to heads of state, and what he coyly described as "suggestions to the Treasury" as his soapbox. But despite the energy with which Keynes prosecuted his case, he realized something more was needed – nothing less than a new economic theory which would explain, and solve, "the enormous anomaly of unemployment in a world full of wants."

Keynes would utilize the insights gained from his roller-coaster ride on the financial markets to develop a revolutionary theory that accounted for the booms and busts of modern economies. A central contention of Keynes' radical thesis would be that financial markets were not always efficient, and that upheavals in the world of money could lead to disturbances in the real economy. As a not unwelcome incidental, Keynes would also alight on a set of investment principles – one of the earliest formulations of the value investing philosophy subsequently adopted by the likes of Warren Buffett – that would propel him to immense wealth. Like his contemporary Irving Fisher, Keynes had been financially mauled by the volatile markets of the late 1920s. Unlike the unfortunate Fisher, however, Keynes would emerge from the slump with his professional reputation burnished and his riches even greater.

5.

RAISING A DUST

INTO THE DAYLIGHT

> *The problem of want and poverty and the economic struggle between classes and nations is nothing but a frightful muddle, a transitory and an unnecessary muddle.*
>
> —Keynes, *Essays in Persuasion*

IN 1930 – AS STOCK MARKETS faltered, dole queues lengthened, and dark clouds of despair shadowed the Western world – John Maynard Keynes, in a characteristically contrarian mood, proffered a vision of civilization one hundred years hence. He invoked a world where, due to the supreme efficiency of the capitalist system, the "struggle for subsistence" has been overcome and man has at last been led "out of the tunnel of economic necessity into daylight." In this utopia, economists are at last relegated to their proper place in society – "as humble, competent people, on a level with dentists," mere technocrats piloting with a delicate touch the ship of state.

Keynes predicted that when this economic Eden has finally been reached:

> We shall be able to rid ourselves of many of the pseudo-moral principles which have hag-ridden us for two hundred years, by which we have exalted some of the most distasteful of human qualities into the position of the highest virtues.

For Keynes, the cult of capitalism fostered a bizarre parallel universe of inverted values, sanctifying some of man's least attractive tendencies – "avarice and usury and precaution" – into a credo for society. He accepted, however, that the means justified the ends – "wisely managed, [capitalism] can probably be made more efficient for attaining economic ends than any alternative system yet in sight." Keynes' attitude to capitalism was rather like that of Churchill's to democracy – the worst system ever invented, except for all the others. It was a necessary crutch until man finally reached the sunlit uplands of abundance, upon which time a more noble means of administering society could be implemented.

Capitalism's chief virtue, and saving grace, had been its efficacy. If the free market system relinquished its claim to matchless productivity there was a danger that other, ostensibly less morally repugnant, social models would be preferred. As Keynes observed:

> Modern capitalism is absolutely irreligious, without internal union, without much public spirit, often, though not always, a mere congeries of possessors and pursuers. Such a system has to be immensely, not merely moderately, successful to survive.

The apparent failure of the free market system to "deliver the goods," Keynes noted in 1933, meant that Western nations were increasingly willing to abandon their Faustian pact with capitalism and instead embark "on a variety of politico-economic experiments."

Despite his own antipathy to many aspects of the system, Keynes believed that capitalism was not fatally flawed. The profound problems of chronic unemployment and economic stagnation had a simple cause, he asserted, and were amenable to a simple remedy. All that was required was to dethrone the existing orthodoxy, and to ground a new theory more firmly in the realities of everyday economic life – an environment in which individuals grappled with an uncertain future and were prey to greed, fear, and irrationality.

CASTING OUT THE MONEY CHANGERS

> *There is always an easy solution to every human problem – neat, plausible, and wrong.*
>
> —H. L. Mencken, *Prejudices*

In March 1933, the recently installed leader of a great but humbled nation addressed his countrymen for the first time in his new capacity. Like an Old Testament firebrand, the leader fulminated against the men of finance who had imperiled his beloved country:

> The money changers have fled from their high seats in the temple of our civilization. We may now restore that temple to the ancient truths. The measure of the restoration lies in the extent to which we apply social values more noble than mere monetary profit.

Noting that "this Nation asks for action, and action now," he urged his compatriots to "move as a trained and loyal army willing to sacrifice for the good of a common discipline ... because it makes possible a leadership which aims at a larger good." If the national emergency remained critical, the leader cautioned, he would seek "broad Executive power ... as great as the power that would be given to me if we were in fact invaded by a foreign foe."

Franklin Delano Roosevelt's Inaugural Address as President of the United States was delivered in the depths of the Depression – when, as FDR observed apocalyptically, "the withered leaves of industrial enterprise lie on every side ... [and] the savings of many years in thousands of families are gone." It disturbingly echoed the messianic platform of the German Nazi Party, which, just two days after Roosevelt's inauguration, garnered the largest number of votes in the country's last free election before the Second World War. The Western world was becoming increasingly desperate – the capitalist system that had served it so well now seemed irremediably broken, and only extreme measures appeared capable of tearing it from its torpor.

This sense of despondency was deepened by the apparent triumphs of Soviet Russia, the country that had most emphatically broken with the free market. Under the uncompromising Five Year Plans issued from the Kremlin, the Soviet Union massively increased its industrial output in the 1930s, almost quadrupling its share of global manufactured products. Seduced by communism's fraternal ideals and its material successes, and perhaps unaware of the human suffering that underwrote these achievements, many of Keynes' friends and students turned "Bolshie" in the Depression decade. Others – generally those in the City or Whitehall – instead sought refuge in the stern, reassuring order of corporatism or fascism. Although the Bolsheviks, the Colonel Blimps, and the Blackshirts squared-off from different ends of the political spectrum, they did have one thing in common – a conviction that the free enterprise system no longer did the job, and needed to be replaced. It seemed, in the mid-1930s, that Marx's grim prognosis of the inbuilt obsolescence of capitalism may have been correct after all.

A NEW WISDOM

> *Half of the copybook wisdom of our statesmen is based upon assumptions that were at one time true, or partly true, but are now less and less true by the day. We have to invent new wisdom for a new age.*
>
> —Keynes, *Essays in Persuasion*

Keynes was not impressed by the arguments of those wishing to depose capitalism. He seemed to regard communism as more Groucho Marx than Karl Marx, dismissing it as "complicated hocus-pocus" and remarking to his students that he had read *Das Kapital* "as if it were a detective story, trying to find some clue to an idea in it and never succeeding." Similarly, he had no time for fascism as a political solution – Keynes' call to action, he informed the British Fascist leader Oswald Mosley, "was to save the country from [you], not to embrace [you]." In Keynes' opinion, the most serious threat to capitalism came not from the aspiring revolutionaries peddling their "quack remedies," but rather from those who most strenuously proclaimed their fealty to the existing order.

Orthodox finance argued that just as in hard times a household should exercise strict financial discipline, so, too, should slump-afflicted governments practice financial sobriety. As Adam Smith reasoned, "What is prudence in the conduct of every private family, can scarce be folly in that of a great kingdom," and conventional wisdom merely extrapolated good housekeeping to the national arena. Backing up orthodoxy's intuitions were the maxims of classical economics, which posited that the free market system benefited from a system of checks and balances that ensured that the economy always tended toward full employment.

In the Panglossian world of classical theory, all savings would be invested, all workers employed, and all products consumed. Consequently, as Keynes remarked, any interference with this self-adjusting system was viewed as:

> not merely inexpedient, but impious, as calculated to retard the onward movement of the mighty process by which we ourselves had risen like Aphrodite out of the primeval slime of ocean.

However, like the Greek philosopher Thales, who stumbled into a well while gazing at the stars, classical fundamentalists were so dazzled by the beauty of their theoretical superstructure that they disregarded the inadequacies of its foundations. Keynes argued that classical theory's "tacit assumptions are seldom or never satisfied, with the result that it cannot solve the economic problems of the actual world." Rather than reprimand reality for failing to live up to the exacting standards of theory, Keynes would develop a model that embraced and explained real-world imperfections.

BOWLING OVER THE FROCK COATS

All successful revolutions are the kicking in of a rotten door.

—John Kenneth Galbraith, *The Age of Uncertainty*

Keynes, the proud iconoclast, was never one to be fettered by the accepted economic verities. He exhibited the underrated English virtue of pragmatism, of not being too tightly wed to any particular view – as he airily informed a Parliamentary Committee in 1930, "I am afraid of 'principle.'" Keynes maintained that economics "is a technique of thinking … not a body of settled conclusions." Although originally a zealous defender of the classical tradition, by the mid-1920s he increasingly ranged himself with the "cranks," asserting that a free market economy could stall at "underemployment equilibrium" for lengthy periods.

Keynes observed that classical economics – built on an assumption of scarcity of resources – was poorly equipped to deal with the situation of excess, squandered resources. The orthodoxy, he stated, "has ruled over us rather by hereditary right than by personal merit," and its policy prescriptions often confounded common sense. Keynes mercilessly attacked the "timidities and mental confusions of the so-called 'sound' finance" – those who recited, as if by rote, the tired tenets of classical theory in support of a policy of financial rectitude and caution:

> When we have unemployed men and unemployed plant ... it is utterly imbecile to say that we cannot *afford* these things. *For it is with the unemployed men and the unemployed plant, and with nothing else, that these things are done.*

Assailing the "deadhead" liquidationists, Keynes argued that the classical paradigm was not inviolate, was not Holy Writ, and by extension the slump was not akin to an Act of God – it was a human problem, and could be solved by the application of sound thinking and courageous initiatives. As Keynes declared in late 1934, "We are ... at one of those uncommon junctures of human affairs where we can be saved by the solution of an intellectual problem, and in no other way." In arriving at a solution to the overwhelming social problem of his time, Keynes would jettison many of the assumptions and conclusions underwriting classical theory. As he declared to a radio audience:

> There is no reason why we should not feel ourselves free to be bold, to be open, to experiment, to take action, to try the possibilities of things. And over against us, standing in the path, there is nothing but a few old gentlemen tightly buttoned-up in their frock coats, who only need to be treated with a little friendly disrespect and bowled over like ninepins.

THE GENERAL THEORY

> *I want, so to speak, to raise a dust; because it is only out of the controversy that will arise that what I am saying will get understood.*
>
> —Keynes to a fellow economist, August 27, 1935

The General Theory of Employment, Interest and Money, published in February 1936, disputed the orthodox doctrine that free markets always produce optimal results. Like its namesake, Einstein's General Theory of Relativity, Keynes' magnum opus overthrew the accepted theoretical structure, showing that markets were not necessarily analogous to the clockwork precision of Newtonian physics. Keynes likened classical economists to "Euclidean geometers in a non-Euclidean world who, discovering that in experience straight lines apparently parallel often meet, rebuke the lines for not keeping straight." In his opinion, parts of the classical doctrine, although theoretically elegant, were based on flawed assumptions and deduced outcomes clearly diverging from those in the real world. Keynes set himself the task of overturning the redundant truths of his predecessors. As he prophesied to his friend George Bernard Shaw in 1935, *The General Theory* would "largely revolutionize ... the way the world thinks about economic problems."

The General Theory was written at a time when most of the developed world had already endured years of chronic unemployment and stagnation – a situation that orthodox economic doctrine deigned impossible, as theory dictated that markets were self-correcting and naturally worked toward full employment. Classical economists argued that the economy was languishing partly because workers were not sufficiently flexible – if only they would behave more like the rational automatons of classical economic theory, willing to take a cut in wages sufficient to justify their employment, then the labor market would self-correct and full employment return.

Keynes believed the orthodox theory – which essentially blamed the unemployed for their plight – to be "wicked" and, moreover, wrong-headed. A central conclusion in *The General Theory* – informed by Keynes' own experience as a speculator – was that the psychology of uncertainty impaired the efficient operation of the market. The existence of uncertainty would periodically result in bouts of underinvestment and oversaving, leading in turn to underutilization of an economy's resources. The Keynesian solution to this state of affairs was, in essence, to boost an economy's aggregate expenditure by increasing government spending to offset lower business and consumer activity.

MONEY MATTERS

Speculation improved his economics and economics improved his speculation.

—Nicholas Davenport on Keynes, *Memoirs of a City Radical*

In the same way that Adam Smith thought that the "vain and insatiable desires" of consumers led by the operation of an invisible hand to the advancement of society as a whole, so, too, did Keynes propose a type of hidden hand which transformed the perceived vices of deficit financing into the virtues of full employment and economic stability. In challenging the paradoxical doctrine of the invisible hand, Keynes, the great perverter, proposed an equally counterintuitive proposal – that at certain times, state profligacy could be the most responsible policy. This idea was deeply offensive to the laissez-faire orthodoxy and to the precepts of sound finance, which clung rigidly to balanced budgets and the principle that expenses should not outrun revenue. Russell Leffingwell, an American banker who had known Keynes since the days of the Paris Peace Conference, typified the City's condescending response to his ideas:

> Keynes and all his school ... have not the judgment of practical men ... They are civil servants. They are professors of political economy. They are not bankers and they are not business men.

In fact, it was precisely because Keynes was more than just a civil servant or economist that he could break free from the orthodox mindset and develop a theory to explain persistent underemployment, for it was Keynes' experiences on the financial markets that gave him an insight into the true workings of modern economies. Traditional theory had largely overlooked the importance of money and financial exchanges – in the classical realm they were little more than conduits, a veil over "real economy" processes. As the Scottish philosopher David Hume had summarized two centuries before, money in orthodox theory is "none of the wheels of trade: It is the oil which renders the motion of the wheels more smooth and easy."

Rather than abstracting money and financial markets from economic theory, Keynes saw them as a driving force. He realized that money was far more than a medium of exchange or the insubstantial shadow of real economy activities – it was "above all, a subtle device for linking the present to the future." Keynes noted that:

> our desire to hold Money as a store of wealth is a barometer of the degree of our distrust of our own calculations and conventions concerning the future. The possession of actual money lulls our disquietude; and the premium which we require to make us part with money is the measure of the degree of our disquietude.

"Liquidity preference" – the desire to hold cash or near-cash – is a gauge of individuals' wariness about the future. When money moves from "industrial circulation" to "financial circulation" – when, rather than being invested in enterprise, savings instead lie fallow – slumps can occur. The flow of money can be thought of as an economy's metabolism, and when individuals hoard their savings because of fears for the future, or when investors lack confidence to embark on new projects, the daisy chain of prosperity breaks and "enterprise will fade and die."

SPENDER OF LAST RESORT

> *This is not a crisis of poverty, but a crisis of abundance. The voices which – in such a conjuncture – tell us that the path of escape is to be found in strict economy and in refraining, wherever possible, from utilizing the world's potential production are the voices of fools and madmen.*
>
> —Keynes, *The World's Economic Outlook*

Rather than having complex and profound causes requiring a radical remedy, Keynes argued that the protracted slump had a simple cause and was capable of a simple solution. The economic engine, he asserted, was suffering from nothing more than "magneto trouble." The motor was largely sound and there was plenty of fuel in reserve – all that was required was a transforming spark to kick-start the machine and return it to the road to prosperity. In the depths of the Great Slump, Keynes buoyantly informed radio listeners that "we are suffering from the growing pains of youth, not from the rheumatics of old age." The celebrated invisible hand, Keynes implied to his audience, merely needed a helping hand.

Like the humanists of an earlier age who rejected the notion of man as a passive plaything of God's will, the Keynesian prescription did not abdicate responsibility for economic welfare to an omniscient, all powerful market. Rather, man's economic destiny was firmly within his own hands – governments could actively intervene to smooth the business cycle by "spending against the wind," as Keynes termed fiscal fine-tuning. As he declared:

> The important thing for government is not to do things which individuals are doing already, and to do them a little better or a little worse; but to do those things which at present are not done at all.

The General Theory polarized opinion. Some commentators, although admiring the book's cleverness, believed it to be intellectually flawed, "a farrago of confused sophistication." Arthur Pigou, a Cambridge economics professor, was complimentary in a rather backhanded way. "We have watched an artist firing arrows at the moon," he commented. "Whatever be thought of his marksmanship, we can all admire his virtuosity." Others, such as the Austrian economist Friedrich von Hayek, thought it a first step to the totalitarian states that had developed in Germany and Russia. Keynes robustly rejected "the pessimism of the reactionaries who consider the balance of our economic and social life so precarious that we must risk no experiments." In moderating the excesses of capitalism – by introducing an element of "socialization of investment" – Keynes believed that society would, in effect, be inoculated against the far more serious threats of collectivism and authoritarianism.

Keynes thought his "monetary theory of production" to be "moderately conservative in its implications." The Keynesian blueprint merely advocated an external stimulus – "an impulse, a jolt, an acceleration," as Keynes put it – when Adam Smith's invisible hand becomes atrophied through inaction. Once the economic engine had been reignited and "our central controls succeed in establishing an aggregate volume of output corresponding to full employment as nearly as is practicable," then, he commented, "the classical theory comes into its own again from this point onwards." In the previous century Lord Salisbury had stated that British foreign policy was "to float lazily downstream, occasionally putting out a diplomatic boathook to avoid collisions." Keynes's proposed economic policy was similar in conception but somewhat more vigorous in execution – the government would act as a rudder on the ship of state, guiding the economy out of danger when unemployment and stagnation loomed.

THE MARK OF KEYNES

All truth passes through three stages. First, it is ridiculed. Second, it is violently opposed. Third, it is accepted as being self-evident.

—Arthur Schopenhauer, *On the Wisdom of Life*

Considering that Keynes' theory told many politicians exactly what they wanted to hear – that the path to recovery lay not in austerity but in higher spending and lower taxes – it is somewhat surprising that his ideas took so long to be accepted by policymakers. It would not be until that period of sustained global public expenditure otherwise known as the Second World War that "Keynesianism" – the belief that fiscal policy should be used to fine-tune an economy's "aggregate demand" – usurped the laissez-faire theories of the classical school almost as comprehensively as Darwin's narrative had displaced that of Genesis.

For three decades after the war, as the Western world luxuriated in conditions of "permanent boom," even Keynes' most vehement ideological adversaries reluctantly conceded that "we are all Keynesians now." Keynes had dragged economics, kicking and screaming, into the twentieth century – from a study of choice under conditions of scarcity to a study of choice under conditions of uncertainty, and from an emphasis on microeconomic factors to an emphasis on aggregates. In his own way, he contributed to the Bloomsbury mission to introduce modernism into Western society, for his economics owed perhaps more to Sigmund Freud's conception of the primal mind than to earlier notions of economic rationality and mechanistic order.

The Keynesian hegemony would yield to a counterrevolution of sorts in the 1970s, when conditions of "stagflation" – consistently rising prices in an environment of high unemployment – fostered the revival of neoclassical economics in general, and monetarism in particular. But just as the embers of the first Keynesian coup were flickering out, a second Keynesian revolution was being kindled. In the late 1970s, the emerging discipline of behavioral finance – a melding of economics and psychology – rediscovered Keynes' views on investor sentiment and stock market dynamics. Having comprehensively overthrown many of the confident conclusions of classical economics during the greatest slump in history, *The General Theory* – perhaps the world's first major work on behavioral economics – would once again prove a foundation text for new ways of thinking.

6.

ANIMAL SPIRITS

WHAT GOES UP . . .

> *To every action there is always opposed an equal reaction.*
>
> —Sir Isaac Newton, *Philosophiae Naturalis Principia Mathematica*

IN JULY 1936, ONLY a few months after the release of *The General Theory*, Keynes acquired at auction a large steel trunk from a financially embattled English aristocrat. The box contained some of the personal papers of Isaac Newton, Cambridge's most famous son. Newton is venerated as a giant of science, the son of an illiterate farmer who ushered the world into the Age of Enlightenment. In the words of Alexander Pope:

> Nature and Nature's laws lay hid in night: God said, Let Newton be! and all was light.

In the year 1666 alone – the "Year of Wonders" – the young Newton, locked away at home after the Plague had forced the closure of Cambridge's colleges, invented differential calculus, formulated the Law of Universal Gravitation, and proposed his Theory of Light. He was celebrated as the discoverer of "the grand secret of the whole Machine," a man whose incandescent intelligence snuffed out the shadows of medieval superstition and ignorance.

The High Priest of Reason was, however, something of a heretic behind closed doors. Much of Newton's early life was spent in his "elaboratory," where, according to his assistant, his "chemical experiments ... aimed at something beyond the reach of human art and industry." Newton was no dry geometer of the universe – despite the mechanistic conception of the world he propounded, he was obsessed with alchemy and the supernatural. He never completely accepted the notion of "inanimate brute matter," suspecting instead that life was invigorated by unseen "animal spirits" in the ether.

Newton was also an ardent pursuer of material wealth. Unsuccessful in his alchemical effort to transmute base metals into gold, he eventually found his own Philosopher's Stone as Master of the Royal Mint. In this capacity, Newton oversaw the recoinage of England's currency, receiving a commission on all coins struck under his supervision and becoming extraordinarily rich in the process. In 1720, toward the end of his long life, Newton ventured some of his fortune in stock of the South Sea Company. After selling his initial holding for a considerable profit, Newton was induced by rising stock prices to re-enter the market. The second time around he was not so lucky. The South Sea Bubble burst and Newton lost around £20,000 – more than $6 million in today's money. Chastened by this demonstration of gravity in the world of finance, he remarked ruefully, "I can calculate the motions of heavenly bodies, but not the madness of people."

Like his hero Newton, Maynard Keynes also learned the hard way that – largely due to the unavoidable fact of uncertainty – financial markets were sometimes buffeted by unpredictable squalls of "whim or sentiment or chance" and prey to "purely irrational waves of optimism or depression." Having spent a decade trying to anticipate the quicksilver tacks of the market, and having been wrong-footed on more than one occasion, Keynes finally concluded that those who run with the crowd are apt to be trampled. Better to stand back from the thundering herd, he decided, than be torn asunder in the running of the bulls or the flight from the bears.

THE UNCERTAINTY PRINCIPLE

> *In the greatest part of our Concernment, [God] has afforded us only the twilight.*
>
> —John Locke, *An Essay Concerning Human Understanding*

Among his other accomplishments, Keynes was also a leading authority on Newton, a position enhanced by his acquisition of the scientist's papers. Keynes brought to the world's attention the occult-obsessed, metaphysical side of Newton – portraying him as a man with "one foot in the Middle Ages, and one foot treading a path for modern science." He also appropriated Newton's idea of "animal spirits" – arguing that in the supposedly mechanistic world of financial markets, investors were often propelled by something other than a clinical analysis of expected outcomes.

Keynes' *General Theory* explained that financial markets are not only prone to periodic informational cascades that compromise efficiency, but also that investors cannot be the rational actors of classical theory because a cold calculation of expected outcomes is simply not possible. With incontrovertible common sense, Keynes observed that there are some events for which "there is no scientific basis on which to form any calculable probability whatever":

> The outstanding fact is the extreme precariousness of the basis of knowledge on which our estimates of prospective yield have to be

> made. Our knowledge of the factors which will govern the yield of an investment some years hence is usually very slight and often negligible. If we speak frankly, we have to admit that our basis of knowledge for estimating the yield ten years hence of a railway, a copper mine, a textile factory, the goodwill of a patent medicine, an Atlantic liner, a building in the City of London amounts to little and sometimes to nothing.

"Wishes are fathers to thoughts," Keynes once observed. Remarkably, it seemed that in championing the case for efficient markets, orthodox theory had glossed over the fact that "core risk" – uncertainty that cannot be assigned a probability – precludes a precise calculation of a stock's expected yield. Keynes therefore rejected orthodox theory's blithe assumption that, in valuing a security, financial market participants could perform "a good Benthamite calculation of a series of prospective advantages and disadvantages, each multiplied by its appropriate probability, waiting to be summed." Despite the assumptions of classical theory, there are, as Keynes pointed out, many factors about which "we simply do not know."

MY INDECISION IS FINAL

> *Prediction is very difficult, especially about the future.*
>
> —Niels Bohr (attributed)

Keynes invoked a paradox beloved of philosophers – that of "Buridan's ass" – to illustrate why "the necessity for action and for decision compels us as practical men" to overlook the "awkward fact" that a uniquely correct valuation of a stock is impossible. Buridan's ass is an apocryphal beast that, faced with two equally attractive and accessible bales of hay, starved while deliberating which one was preferable. Like the donkey of the parable, stock market participants – if they were to attempt to apply a purely rational approach to their investment decisions – would also be rendered immobile by the daunting "what ifs" of an unknowable future. Instead, they resort to less analytical factors when assessing stock market opportunities:

> To avoid being in the position of Buridan's ass, we fall back ... on motives ... which are not "rational" in the sense of being concerned with the evaluation of consequences, but are decided by habit, instinct, preference, desire, will etc.

The stock market player is impelled – in part at least – by factors that, although not rational, are nevertheless legitimate in some sense. Unlike the situation with, say, government bonds – which pay a fixed coupon, and whose present investment value can be determined with reasonable precision – stocks exist in a twilight zone of ambiguity. This uncertainty gap is a blank canvas on which the investor projects his or her most fervent hopes or darkest fears. "Animal spirits" – the "spontaneous urge to action rather than inaction," as Keynes defined them – embolden individuals and allow them to bridge the uncertainty gap inherent in any investment decision.

The investor, Keynes concluded, is not the perfectly knowledgeable calculating machine of orthodox theory. Despite the assertions of efficient markets proponents, stock market behavior is not – *cannot be* – governed by purely rational factors. *Investor psychology* plays an integral role in the decision to buy, sell, or hold a stock. As Keynes summarized:

> a large proportion of our positive activities depend on spontaneous optimism rather than on a mathematical expectation, whether moral or hedonistic or economic. Most, probably, of our decisions to do something positive, the full consequences of which will be

> drawn out over many days to come, can only be taken as a result of animal spirits and not as the outcome of a weighted average of quantitative benefits multiplied by quantitative probabilities.

JUMPING AT SHADOWS

> *The stock market has predicted nine out of the last five recessions.*
>
> —Paul Samuelson, *Newsweek*

Not only does the presence of uncertainty mean that investors fall back on their "state of confidence" or "animal spirits" when making investment decisions, but it also exaggerates the impact of near-term factors on a stock's performance. In his *A Treatise on Money*, published in 1930, Keynes noted:

> how sensitive – over-sensitive if you like – to the near future, about which we may think we know a little, even the best-informed must be, because, in truth, we know almost nothing about the more remote future.

Not unreasonably, Keynes conceded, investors attach greater weight to matters about which they are relatively more confident, "even though they may be less decisively relevant to the issue than other facts about which our knowledge is vague and scanty." In consequence:

> the facts of the existing situation enter, in a sense disproportionately, into the formation of our long-term expectations; our usual practice being to take the existing situation and to project it into the future, modified only to the extent that we have more or less definite reasons for expecting a change.

The broad assumption that "the existing state of affairs will continue indefinitely" means that:

> Day-to-day fluctuations in the profits of existing investments, which are obviously of an ephemeral and non-significant character, tend to have an altogether excessive, and even an absurd, influence on the market.

As an example of this tendency, Keynes claimed – not without a touch of hyperbole – that "the shares of American companies which manufacture ice tend to sell at a higher price in summer when their profits are seasonally high than in winter when no one wants ice" and that the "recurrence of a bank-holiday may raise the market valuation of the British railway system by several million pounds."

The focus on the shorter term means that investor expectations – and therefore stock prices – are extremely sensitive to new information, and that:

> Faced with the perplexities and uncertainties of the modern world, market values will fluctuate much more widely than will seem reasonable in the light of after-events.

In simple terms, the unavoidable fact of uncertainty prompts stock market players to latch on to new information, causing stock prices to overshoot. Empirical evidence supports Keynes' thesis – studies show that stock prices display far greater volatility than would be expected relative to changes in underlying earnings and dividends. Exacerbating this tendency to overweight new information is the "risk averse" nature of the average investor – his or her propensity to feel financial losses more keenly than equivalent gains. Risk aversion may cause stock prices to react disproportionately to negative news, as investors overdiscount security prices affected by unfavorable new information.

CONFIDENCE TRICK

Reasoning will never make a man correct an ill opinion, which by reasoning he never acquired.

—Jonathan Swift

The stock market, Keynes demonstrated, was not always the unassailable paragon of efficiency that orthodox financial theorists claimed it to be. It was prone to informational cascades – episodes where prices would snowball in one direction or the other merely because momentum had seized the market – and, more fundamentally, investment decisions were impelled to some extent by necessarily non-rational factors. As Keynes pointed out, due to the inescapable fact of uncertainty, "all sorts of considerations enter into the market valuation which are in no way relevant to the prospective yield."

To take but one example, a biographer of Marcel Proust, that rich but troubled neurasthenic of the early twentieth century, noted that the French author:

> made many ruinous investments but refused to listen to his banker . . . More often than not he purchased a stock because of its poetic name ("The Tanganyika Railway," "The Australian Gold Mines"); in fact, these stocks were a substitute for the travels to exotic places he longed to make.

Like Tolstoy's unhappy families, all irrational investors are irrational in their own particular way. Proust's purchases, made in the antiseptic emptiness of his cork-lined bedroom, were guided by the evocativeness of a company name, their words as charged with associations as his tea-soaked madeleine biscuits. Other, perhaps less poetically inclined, market players might equally be influenced by a perceived trend in a stock's price, a compelling foundation story, or what the chap next door is doing.

Keynes' view of the stock market was diametrically opposed to that of orthodox financial theory, where, as the reference books inform the reader, "investors are unromantically concerned with the firm's cash flows and the portion of those cash flows to which they are entitled." In the make-believe world of classical theory, the stock market was conceived as an infallible machine for crystallizing the present value of future income from a security. Real world complications such as uncertainty and the state of investor confidence were conveniently disregarded in the interests of theoretical elegance. Orthodox theory did not admit the possibility that the virus of animal spirits could infect the machine, causing it to generate numbers which could depart widely from any reasonable assessment of true value.

STATE OF EMERGENCY

> *Under certain circumstances ... an agglomeration of men presents new characteristics very different from those of the individuals comprising it.*
>
> —Gustave Le Bon, *The Crowd*

Economics has been greatly influenced by discoveries in the "hard" sciences – the clockwork precision of Newtonian physics was reflected in classical theory's mechanistic conception of the world; Darwin's doctrine of survival of the fittest inspired the muscular free-trade policies of the Victorian era; and Einstein's bizarre theories of relativity were mirrored in the Keynesian universe, where money – like time – was sometimes more than a mere inert cipher. Keynes argued, however, that economics seemed to depart from the comforting resemblance to science in at least one key respect. In the discipline of economics, he asserted, "the atomic hypothesis that has worked so splendidly in physics breaks down," and consequently:

> We are faced at every turn with the problems of organic unity, of discreteness, of discontinuity – the whole is not equal to the

> sum of the parts, comparisons of quantity fail us, small changes produce large effects, the assumptions of a uniform and homogeneous continuum are not satisfied.

The economy, as Keynes noted, exhibits what have come to be called "emergent properties": complex, sometimes unpredictable, collective behavior in a system, arising out of the multiplicity of interactions between its individual constituents.

Behavior in the atomistic world of microeconomics cannot always be extrapolated to the sphere of macroeconomics, the study of aggregates. Keynes' most famous example of the "fallacy of composition" was the so-called Paradox of Thrift – which notes that saving is good for the individual, but if all individuals increase their savings then aggregate demand will fall, eventually leading to lower savings for the population as a whole. Similarly, the stock market – one of the purest expressions of the free market system – can, on occasions, display emergent properties, where individual behavior mutates into mob irrationality. Even for someone of Keynes' protean interests and abilities, the stock market was simply too vast and too complex a mechanism to second-guess.

A SENTIMENTAL EDUCATION

> *Don't try to buy at the bottom and sell at the top. This cannot be done – except by liars.*
>
> —Bernard Baruch, *My Own Story*

Keynes eventually concluded that because of the utter capriciousness and complexity of the stock market, a short-term "momentum investing" approach rarely rewarded its followers with financial success. As he conceded to a colleague in May 1938:

> I can only say that I was the principal inventor of credit cycle investment and have seen it tried by five different parties acting in detail on distinctly different lines over a period of nearly twenty years, which has been full of ups and downs; and I have not seen a single case of a success having been made of it.

Keynes thought that credit cycling not only demanded "abnormal foresight" and required "phenomenal skill to make much out of it," but that transaction expenses from such a necessarily active investment policy tended to erode trading profits. He expanded on this theme in a memorandum to the King's College Estates Committee:

> I am clear that the idea of wholesale shifts [out of and into stocks at different stages of the business cycle] is for various reasons impracticable and indeed undesirable. Most of those who attempt it sell too late and buy too late, and do both too often, incurring heavy expenses and developing too unsettled and speculative a state of mind.

Keynes' realization that there was no method to the market's madness prompted a radical change in his investment approach. Following the Great Crash, he completely inverted his investment principles, becoming an investor rather than a speculator – one who focuses on likely future performance rather than past trends, expected yield rather than disposal price, particular stocks rather than the broader index, and relying on his own judgment rather than that of the market. Simply stated, Keynes switched from market timer to value investor, seeking to profit from swings in the market rather than participating in them.

7.

GAME PLAYERS

FLOWERING INFERNO

> *"It's always best on these occasions to do what the mob do." "But suppose there are two mobs?" suggested Mr. Snodgrass. "Shout with the largest," replied Mr. Pickwick.*
>
> —Charles Dickens, *The Pickwick Papers*

"TULIPOMANIA" SAW THE PATHOGEN of animal spirits visit that most stolid of people, the Dutch burghers of the seventeenth century. As Charles Mackay recalls in his catalog of human folly, *Extraordinary Popular Delusions and the Madness of Crowds,* the "rage to possess" tulips was so powerful that:

> Nobles, citizens, farmers, mechanics, seamen, footmen, maidservants, even chimney-sweeps and old clotheswomen, dabbled in tulips. People of all grades converted their property in cash, and invested it in flowers.

Speculative fervor for the exotic plants was such that traders, in an early version of a futures contract, started to sell the rights to bulbs they had not yet even planted. This innovation – dismissively labeled *windhandel,* or "wind trade," by those untouched by the mania – encouraged even more speculation, as trading moved from the physical to the abstract.

"Broken" flowers – cultivars with flares of blazing color – were the most highly valued. By early 1637, one bulb of the *Semper Augustus* strain – its blood-red flames vivid against a pure white – commanded the same price as a large canal-side house in Amsterdam. The variegated hues of these prized flowers were caused by a virus, and, as was later discovered, it was the virus that both increased the attractiveness of the flowers and also contributed to their frailty. As Mackay explained:

> When it has been weakened by cultivation, [the tulip] becomes more agreeable in the eyes of the florist ... Thus this masterpiece of culture, the more beautiful it turns, grows so much the weaker, so that, with the greatest skill and most careful attention, it can scarcely be transplanted, or even kept alive.

The Dutch tulipomania eventually, and inevitably, unwound in a most spectacular manner. Bulbs that had sold for 5,000 guilders in January 1637 fetched only 50 guilders a month later. The Dutch courts correctly diagnosed the malady that had temporarily seized the population – characterizing the transactions as nothing more than gambling operations, they declined to enforce outstanding contracts of sale.

The tulipomania – in addition to providing another illustration of the periodic irrationality that ensnares markets – also affords a metaphor for financial exchanges generally. Like the tulip, whose refinement and frailty move in tandem, the more highly evolved a stock market, the greater the risk that it will be susceptible to the contagion of animal spirits. As Keynes noted in *The General Theory,* when "the organization of investment markets improves, the risk of the predominance of speculation does, however, increase."

Having disposed of the fiction of investors as rational calculating machines summing risk-weighted expected cash flows, Keynes then proceeded in *The General Theory* to identify other factors, largely attributable to the increasing sophistication of financial exchanges, that he believed compromised the efficiency of markets. When discriminating investors are "so much in the minority that their behavior does not govern the market," Keynes argued, a stock exchange could assume the traits of its "game players," evincing an excessively short-term approach and presenting with bipolar tendencies.

THE DANGERS OF DEMOCRACY

> *I don't want to belong to any club that will accept me as a member.*
>
> —Groucho Marx, *Groucho and Me*

Keynes, unapologetic elitist that he was, believed that the increasing democratization of stock investing adversely affected the stability of the system. As he observed in *The General Theory*:

> That the sins of the London Stock Exchange are less than those of Wall Street may be due, not so much to differences in national character, as to the fact that to the average Englishman Throgmorton Street is, compared with Wall Street to the average American, inaccessible and very expensive.

Keynes thought that "liquid" financial exchanges – those with low transaction costs and that are effectively open to all – encouraged the entry of dilettante investors who "have no special knowledge of the circumstances, either actual or prospective, of the business in question."

He believed that the lack of real knowledge about the underlying business increased the stock market's fickleness and its propensity to overreact to new information, "since there will be no strong roots of conviction to hold [a valuation] steady." Keynes also lamented that the financial exchanges – with their constant price quotations and potential to readily monetize investments – gave:

> a frequent opportunity to the individual ... to revise his commitments. It is as though a farmer, having tapped his barometer after breakfast, could decide to remove his capital from the farming business between 10 and 11 in the morning and reconsider whether he should return to it later in the week.

Greater liquidity, lower or zero transaction costs, and the advent of the internet and handheld devices combine to make shares even easier to trade today, and in consequence have further exacerbated the flightiness of capital. These factors also make stocks increasingly abstract concepts, disembodied from the businesses they represent – "an abstraction, a name, a symbol interchangeable with a certain amount of money," as one commentator described the transformation of the humble tulip during the Dutch derangement of the seventeenth century. The perception by many market participants that stocks are little more than a number on a computer screen or an icon on a smartphone – a mere trading chip divorced from the underlying business, rather than a part-interest in the business itself – further inflames the speculative mindset.

OUTRUNNING THE BEAR

> *Worldly wisdom teaches that it is better for reputation to fail conventionally than to succeed unconventionally.*
>
> —Keynes, *The General Theory*

The story is told of two hunters, madly scrambling through a forest, trying to evade a particularly cantankerous and agile bear. Mid-pursuit, one stops, reaches into his backpack, and changes into running shoes. The other man tells him he is crazy – there is no way he will be able to outrun the bear, even with his new footwear. "I don't need to outrun the bear," he replies, "I just need to outrun *you*." A similar dynamic exists on modern stock markets, where fund managers and other financial institutions are largely assessed on performance relative to their peers over short intervals, rather than by reference to their absolute investment performance over the longer term. This benchmarking practice naturally encourages fund managers to adopt a near-term focus – for even if the institutions themselves are impervious to the siren calls of the mob, their unit-holders may not possess the same forbearance.

The efficient markets hypothesis states that although some stock market participants may not boast Spock-like levels of rationality and cool-headedness, the smart money will nevertheless act to rein in any pricing anomalies produced. Keynes dismissed this belief as little more than a convenient fiction:

> It might have been supposed that competition between expert professionals, possessing judgment and knowledge beyond that of the average private investor, would correct the vagaries of the ignorant individual left to himself. It happens, however, that the energies and skill of the professional investor and speculator are mainly occupied otherwise. For most of these persons are, in fact, largely concerned, not with making superior long-term forecasts of the probable yield of an investment over its whole life, but with foreseeing changes in the conventional basis of valuation a short time ahead of the general public.

Professional investors, in practice, rarely accept the role of market monitor assigned to them by orthodox theory. As Keynes noted, there is overwhelming institutional pressure to conform, even among allegedly sophisticated investors:

> it is the long-term investor, he who most promotes the public interest, who will in practice come in for most criticism, wherever investment funds are managed by committees or boards or banks. For it is in the essence of his behavior that he should be eccentric, unconventional and rash in the eyes of average opinion. If he is successful, that will only confirm the general belief in his rashness; and if in the short run he is unsuccessful, which is very likely, he will not receive much mercy.

Like the mass of investors, fund managers are more often concerned with not underperforming than trying to outperform. In practice, they do not provide a countervailing force against the more flighty investors – indeed, on many occasions they actually amplify the swings of investor irrationality.

Intensifying the short-term focus of many institutional investment managers are two additional factors – an emphasis on "total returns" as a performance guide, and the presence of "index-tracking funds." Total returns measures – comprising dividend payments and any increase or decrease in the price of a given stock – are usually dominated by unrealized capital gains or losses, which once again focuses attention on short-term stock price fluctuations. Index-tracking funds – investment vehicles that seek to replicate market performance by holding a representative portfolio of stocks – aggravate the market's tendency to overshoot by reinforcing trends in the market. Index funds are momentum investors *in excelsis* – they automatically buy more of a stock as its price, and therefore its value relative to the broader market, increases, and sell as its price decreases – thus adding to overshoots and further eroding the purported efficiency of financial exchanges.

BIPOLAR BEARS (AND BULLS)

> *[Bipolar Affective Disorder] is ... characterized by repeated ... episodes in which ... mood and activity levels are significantly disturbed, this disturbance consisting on some occasions of an elevation of mood and increased energy and activity (mania ...), and on others of a lowering of mood and decreased energy and activity (depression). Characteristically, recovery is usually complete between episodes.*
>
> —*Classification of Mental and Behavioural Disorders,* World Health Organization

Keynes demonstrated that the stock market could move violently in response to changes in investor psychology, was susceptible to informational cascades, could overshoot based on new information, was excessively focused on near-term price performance, and was populated by investors having "no special knowledge" of the stocks in which they trade. One financial markets practitioner who shared Keynes' rather jaundiced view was Benjamin Graham, an American investor and academic. Like Keynes, Graham had been badly burnt by the Great Crash, his stock portfolio losing almost three-quarters of its value during the slump. And again like Keynes, this loss – combined with observations picked up while working on Wall Street – motivated Graham to think deeply about financial exchanges and their frailties.

Graham believed that stock markets were periodically influenced by pendulum swings of investor sentiment, when quoted prices depart significantly from a stock's underlying value, and that these swings could be exploited by the rational, patient investor:

> price fluctuations have only one significant meaning for the true investor. They provide him with an opportunity to buy wisely when prices fall sharply and to sell wisely when they advance a great deal.

To illustrate his thesis, Ben Graham proposed a novel way to think about the stock market. He encouraged investors to imagine that they are dealing with an individual who, each trading day, offers to buy or sell stocks at a given price. As Graham explained, "Mr. Market"

> is very obliging indeed. Every day he tells you what he thinks your interest is worth and furthermore offers either to buy you out or sell you an additional interest on that basis.

Mr. Market is often a relatively stable and rational entity, offering to deal in stocks at prices which approximate their true worth. Sometimes, however, Mr. Market lapses into mania or depression, is panicked by a negative piece of news or elated by apparently positive developments, or focuses excessively on short-term factors while missing the bigger picture. When Mr. Market "lets his enthusiasm or his fears run away with him," Graham observed, "the value he proposes seems to you a little short of silly."

The stock market, Graham implied, could sometimes be neurotic, paranoid, myopic, and afflicted by mania or depression – if it were an individual, it would be medicated. Yet despite all his pathologies and character flaws, Mr. Market possesses one sterling virtue – that of perseverance. He is not offended if an investor is unresponsive to his constant solicitations, and will unfailingly return every trading day with renewed offers to buy and sell securities. Using Mr. Market as an investment adviser, Graham cautioned, could be ruinous for an investor. On the other hand, the poor fellow could be exploited when he was in the throes of an irrational episode – for although Mr. Market frequently degenerated into a form of madness, he would eventually come to his senses, and stock prices would in due course revert toward their fundamental value.

ALPHA BETS

Charlie Munger: If you mix raisins with turds, they're still turds.
Warren Buffett: That's why they have me write the annual report.
—Berkshire Hathaway annual meeting, 2000

Ben Graham's investment company spawned a number of highly successful value investors, the most famous of whom is Warren Buffett. Buffett is one of the world's richest men, but unlike most other members of the billionaires' club, his wealth was built entirely from stock market and other company investments. As *Time* magazine noted in a profile on Buffett:

> We've seen oil magnates, real estate moguls, shippers, and robber barons at the top of the money heap, but Buffett is the first person to get there just by picking stocks.

Buffett has been investing for many decades, and his record is remarkable. Since he acquired Berkshire Hathaway as his investment vehicle over half a century ago, the company has outperformed the broader market by more than a hundred-fold margin. This investment performance represents an average compounded return of around 20 per cent a year – a record unmatched by any other large, long-term investor.

Buffett and his vice chairman at Berkshire Hathaway, Charles Munger, are the Butch Cassidy and Sundance Kid of the investment world. Buffett is a wisecracking, Coke-swigging nonagenarian dispensing pithy financial wisdom in perfectly honed epigrams, while the slightly older Munger revels in the role of straight man and resident curmudgeon. In his letters to stockholders and at Berkshire Hathaway's annual meetings – labeled "Woodstock for Capitalists" by the chairman – Buffett plays up the image of himself as a gauche but deceptively wise Midwesterner, possessed of deep reserves of folksy common sense. The phlegmatic

Buffett is the antithesis of the edgy, volatile stock market players depicted in popular culture, and there is a satisfying moral resonance to his message – the meek and unflashy may indeed inherit the earth.

Warren Buffett is not the "Wizard of Wall Street" or the "Sage of Silicon Valley," but rather the "Oracle of Omaha." Berkshire Hathaway is headquartered in Omaha, Nebraska – about equidistant from Wall Street and Silicon Valley, as if reluctant to get too close to either. The positioning seems uncannily appropriate. The Berkshire Hathaway duo dismiss many of the maxims of conventional finance, and their consistent outperformance of the broader indices is a living reproof to the efficient markets hypothesis. They are proud Luddites, famous abstainers during the dot-com delirium of the late 1990s, and merciless critics of the hyperactivity of day traders and some investment funds. In a feat of exquisite symmetry – and as if to underline Buffett's contrarian investment style and his absolute antipathy to the financial fads that periodically hijack the market – during the rollicking dot-com days of early 2000, Berkshire Hathaway stock fell to a three-year low on the same day the NASDAQ reached its record high.

Buffett owes much of his success to Ben Graham's insights on stock market behavior. He has embraced Graham's Mr. Market analogy – frequently referring to the "various forms of mass hysteria that infect the investment markets from time to time" – and has also wholeheartedly adopted some of Graham's other principles, such as ensuring that a significant "margin of safety" exists when purchasing securities. But in many ways Buffett's stock market philosophy is far closer to that practiced by Keynes decades earlier. Noting that Keynes "began as a market-timer … and converted, after much thought, to value investing," Buffett often cites his philosophical fellow traveler when musing on the stock market.

FAR FROM THE MADDING CROWD

When the facts change, I change my mind – what do you do, sir?

—Keynes (attributed)

Keynes' break with credit cycling marked his transformation from speculator to investor. He defined speculation as "the activity of forecasting the psychology of the market," in contrast to "enterprise," or true investment, which involves "forecasting the prospective yield of assets over their whole life." The investor focuses on the income that a security is expected to produce, not the possible sale price of that security in the near term. Or, to employ Keynes' terminology, the true investor is concerned more with "ultimate values" than "exchange values."

Rather than trying to be a type of market barometer – gauging whether fair winds or foul would visit the exchange – Keynes decided to take advantage of the stock market's "bull tacks" and "bear tacks" in another way. He would no longer attempt to *time*, or anticipate, *general* movements in the market; instead, he would use the *value* of a *particular* stock as his investment guide. Only when the pendulum of investor sentiment had swung too far in respect of a given stock, such that the quoted price veered significantly from assessed fundamental value, would Keynes consider buying or selling that security.

As Keynes summarized, this alternative investment policy:

> assumes the ability to pick specialties which have, on the average, prospects of rising enormously more than an index of market leaders ... [T]his practice does, in my opinion, in fact enable one to take at least as good an advantage of fluctuations as credit cycling, though in a rather different way. It is largely the fluctuations which throw up the bargains and the uncertainty due to fluctuations which prevents other people from taking advantage of them.

Keynes realized that the distance from manic to panic on the stock market could be vanishingly short. Rather than trying to outwit the mercurial mob and anticipate inflections in the investment cycle, he concluded it was far more preferable to pick the low-hanging fruit that occasionally presented itself to the investor.

THE PRODIGAL SON

> *There are two times in a man's life when he should not speculate: when he can't afford it, and when he can.*
>
> —Mark Twain, *Pudd'nhead Wilson's New Calendar*

Keynes' switch from speculator to value investor delivered a radical change in his fortunes. In contrast to the grim days of the early 1930s – where, "although not quite destitute," he had been obliged to put two of his best-loved paintings, a Matisse and a Seurat, up for sale – Keynes had again become "horribly prosperous" by the time *The General Theory* was published. In the years between the Wall Street Crash and the end of 1936, Keynes multiplied his wealth more than sixtyfold, parlaying net assets of just under £8,000 at the end of 1929 to more than £500,000 only six years later.

Just as impressive as his financial recovery was his return to the Establishment fold. The man who had likened himself to Cassandra of Greek mythology – gifted with the powers of prophecy, but fated never to be believed – found himself embraced once again by the ruling elite. Like Churchill, Keynes was drafted to deal with a situation he had long presaged, when in 1940 he became an unpaid adviser to the Chancellor – in his words, a "demi-semi-official" with a wide-ranging brief to formulate economic policy for war-pressed Britain. The following year he was installed as a director of the Bank of England – on his appointment he quipped to his mother that it could only be a matter of time before he became a bishop – and in 1942 elevated to a peerage, becoming Lord Keynes, Baron of Tilton. In the closing stages of the war he continued to straddle the worlds of Mammon and of Art – acting as Britain's chief representative at both the international monetary conference at Bretton Woods and in loan negotiations with the United States, and becoming the United Kingdom's first arts tsar as inaugural chairman of what would evolve into the British Arts Council.

Remarkably, these various offices were carried out while Keynes was in extremely frail health. In mid-1937, just before his fifty-fourth birthday, he suffered his first heart attack, and was confined to a sanatorium and later his country house in Sussex for much of his convalescence. Paralleling Keynes' physical breakdown was a short, sharp economic recession in late 1937 and 1938, accompanied by another severe "sinking spell" on major stock markets. Unable to attend many board and investment committee meetings due to his enforced confinement, and obliged to defend his stock market techniques amid yet another bout of pervasive pessimism, Keynes explained his investment philosophy in a series of letters and memoranda to his colleagues.

It is from this rich documentary legacy that we distill Keynes' six key investment principles, representing a straightforward and time-tested system for exploiting the periodic irrationality of stock markets.

8.

SEARCHING FOR STUNNERS

THE DAMN'D SOUTH SEA

> *The additional rise of this stock above the true capital will be only imaginary; one added to one, by any rules of vulgar arithmetic, will never make three and a half; consequently, all the fictitious value must be a loss to some persons or other, first or last. The only way to prevent it to oneself must be to sell out betimes, and so let the Devil take the hindmost.*
>
> —Unknown contemporary commentator, on the South Sea bubble

THE SOUTH SEA COMPANY, WHEN established in 1711, seemed an elegant solution to a number of disparate problems. It would take over Britain's burgeoning public debt by converting government borrowings into Company equity, its trading rights to Spain's American colonies could be used as a bargaining chip with the belligerent Spanish king, and the venture, if successful, promised to fill the coffers of the Exchequer with substantial trading profits. Yet despite support from the highest levels – King George was appointed Governor of the Company in 1715 – the enterprise initially languished. The "trade monopoly" secured over the Spanish Americas was pitiful, in both senses of the word: an annual quota of 4,800 *piezas de Indias* (male African slaves, no defects, at least 58 inches in height), as well as one ship per year carrying miscellaneous commercial goods. The venture yielded no substantial profit and, in any case, war with Spain in 1718 effectively terminated the trading rights of the Company.

The fortunes of the South Sea Company were, however, reinvigorated in March 1720 when it won a bidding contest against the Bank of England to acquire more government debt in another stock-for-borrowings swap. In an effort to procure a favorable exchange rate for the conversion, promoters talked up the prospects of the Company and circulated "the most extravagant rumors" of the potential value of its trading concessions with the New World. Stock prices rocketed from £128 per share in January 1720 to just over £1,000 less than six months later. Prefiguring day traders' chat rooms of our era, the boosterism of Company directors was abetted by stimulant-stoked gossip in coffee houses and wildly optimistic reports in the newfangled medium of newspapers.

London was caught up in a fetish for easy money. Samuel Johnson later noted that "even poets panted after wealth" – Alexander Pope, he wrote, "ventured some of his money ... and for a while he thought himself the lord of thousands." Although himself caught in the riptide of greed, Pope still had an eye to the deleterious effect of South Sea hysteria, which diverted the populace from the banal, but necessary, responsibilities of everyday life:

> No Ships unload, no Looms at Work we see,
> But all are swallow'd by the damn'd South Sea.

Women, constrained in their dealings in real property, were particularly enthusiastic participants in the stock market frenzy. One lady,

Sarah, Duchess of Marlborough, realized that prices for South Sea stock were not anchored to any bed of true value:

> Every mortal that has common sense or that knows anything of figures, sees that 'tis not possible by all the arts and tricks upon earth long to carry £400,000,000 of paper credit with £15,000,000 of specie. This makes me think that this project must burst in a little while and fall to nothing.

The Duchess – who, her great-grandson Winston Churchill would later remark, possessed an "almost repellent common sense" – sold her shares near the market peak, pocketing the then astronomical sum of £100,000. For the following couple of months, she continued to profit from the mob by extending heavily secured loans to some of her more bullish peers. Ultimately, they did not share the Duchess's good fortune – prompted by the failure of a similar scheme in France, spooked by the closure of trading ports due to the Plague, and perhaps affected by a general credit squeeze, the bubble eventually burst. By December 1720 the stock had sputtered back to ground – describing an almost perfect parabola on the share price chart, South Sea paper traded at exactly the same level as at the start of the year.

As the Duchess of Marlborough shrewdly observed, stock exchanges can at times confect prices which veer considerably from any reasonable estimate of underlying value. Almost three centuries later, despite – and often because of – the sophistication of modern exchanges, stock markets are still prone to episodes in which pricing and value radically diverge. Like the Duchess, Maynard Keynes concluded by the early 1930s that, as one of his biographers put it, "the laws of arithmetic were more reliable than the winds of rumor" – far better, he decided, to ground investment decisions in the firm foundation of hard analysis than in something as impalpable as "market sentiment."

NULLIUS IN VERBA

The seekers after perpetual motion are trying to get something from nothing.

—Sir Isaac Newton (attributed)

In July 1720, the British parliament passed the "Bubble Act," which prohibited the formation of joint stock companies unless expressly authorized by Royal Charter. Although some cynics suggested that the real purpose of the legislation was to allow the South Sea Company to corner the market on investor credulity, the ostensible explanation for the Act was to curb the speculative wildfire ignited by the South Sea bubble. Exploiting the "inordinate thirst of gain that had afflicted all ranks of society" during the mad days of early 1720, other company promoters had attempted to raise money for projects of dubious merit, including a hush-hush enterprise "for carrying on an undertaking of great advantage, but nobody to know what it is," and another to build a wheel for perpetual motion.

Isaac Newton – the practitioner of "cold and untinctured reason" in his scientific endeavors – became the most famous "cully", or victim, of the South Sea hysteria. Perhaps the continued rise of South Sea stock in the summer of 1720 convinced him that the market could simply not be wrong, that Britain had indeed stumbled on a corporate El Dorado. In any case, the man who was once a dirt-poor student among the Cambridge toffs, supporting himself by scrubbing the floors and emptying the bedpans of his more affluent classmates, was beguiled by the vision of abundant wealth shimmering on the horizon. He, like so many others, became intoxicated by the "unwholesome fermentation" produced by the action of animal spirits, in which "the hope of boundless wealth for the morrow made [men] heedless and extravagant for today."

Newton, then the President of the Royal Society, the world's oldest existent academy of science, failed to heed its eminently wise motto,

Nullius in Verba – don't take anyone's word for it. Had he applied the same rigor to his stock speculations as he did to his scientific speculations, Newton would have realized that, just as certain fundamental laws in physics mandate that a perpetual motion machine cannot exist, so too the inexorable rise of South Sea stock could not last. Instead of following the crowd, he would have been far better served exercising "his unusual powers of continuous concentrated introspection," as Keynes characterized what he considered Newton's chief strength. Upon even a cursory analysis, Newton would have concluded that the prices of South Sea shares were levitating entirely as a result of the collective will of speculators, rather than by reference to any economic fundamentals.

THE ECONOMIST AND THE $100 BILL

> *A neoclassical economist and his pupil are sauntering across a university green one day, discussing the finer points of financial theory, when the undergraduate sights what seems to be a $100 bill skipping across the grass. The student quickens his pace to intercept the fugitive note, but the economist indulgently restrains his young charge. "If it really were a $100 bill," the older man advises, "someone would have picked it up by now."*
>
> —Market anecdote

After his own stock market reverses, Keynes determined that value investing – basing the investment decision on a comparison of the likely future returns from a security against its asking price – was the best corrective to the periodic visitations of animal spirits. Value investing repudiates a fundamental tenet of the efficient markets hypothesis by asserting that there can in fact be a sustained divergence between the quoted price of a stock and its underlying value. Value investors are fond of citing the parable of the economist and the $100 bill to parody the "strong form" of the efficient markets theory, which states that there are no hitherto undiscovered bargains – and, conversely, no overpriced lemons – lurking on sophisticated financial exchanges.

As characterized by some financial commentators, an efficient financial market is one in which the sheep are protected from the wolves by other wolves – that is, discerning investors will operate to trim any disparity between quoted price and true worth by bidding up apparently underpriced stocks and selling down overpriced paper. By so doing, these stock market vigilantes – the pike in the carp-pond, to borrow Keynes' metaphor – ensure that, in theory, unsophisticated investors will not be at the mercy of the smart money. As the authors of *Principles of Corporate Finance,* a foundation text in undergraduate finance classes around the world, assure their readers: "In an efficient market you can trust prices. They impound all available information about the value of each security."

Efficient markets proponents will often go to great lengths to defend their theory. They may argue, for example, that the ever-ascending prices of a fervid bull market are justified by a particular innovation or improvement in the economic environment – "This time it's different," they persuade themselves, as old valuation metrics are casually discarded. Former President Herbert Hoover, for instance, recalled the self-serving fictions invented to justify the extravagant stock prices of the late 1920s:

> With the growing optimism, they gave birth to a foolish idea called the "New Economic Era." The notion spread over the whole country. We were assured that we were in a new period where the old laws of economics no longer applied.

Stock market players, it is apparent, are sometimes more adept at rationalization than rationality.

Other adherents to the orthodoxy simply proffer the circular argument that prices must always be correct because they are the product of an all-knowing exchange. The comforting conceit of efficient markets seemingly blinds some to the common sense observation that financial exchanges periodically experience spasms of irrationality, where security prices diverge considerably from any reasonable assessment of underlying value. The backers of the efficient markets hypothesis simply do not accept that on occasions there are not enough wolves to corral the sheep, and that the bleating flock can blindly file into a chasm.

THE WEIGHTING GAME

> *It is impossible to avoid a precipice, when one follows a road that leads nowhere else.*
>
> —Jean-Baptiste Say, *A Treatise on Political Economy*

Efficient markets fundamentalists, in arguing that stock prices *always* incorporate *all* public information impacting the value of a security, succumb to an absurdly basic error. As Warren Buffett has noted:

> Observing correctly that the market was *frequently* efficient, [many academics and investment professionals] went on to conclude incorrectly that it was *always* efficient. The difference between these propositions is night and day.

Value investors, by definition, do not accept the strong form of the efficient markets theory. There are times when the quoted price of a security departs from its underlying value, these investors believe, and it is on these occasions that the intelligent investor seeks to exploit the mispricing that results.

Despite their skepticism about the effectiveness of the stock market in the short run, value investors generally accept that over the longer term stock markets price securities efficiently. As Keynes commented in a letter to a colleague, "when the safety, excellence, and cheapness of a share is generally realized, its price is bound to go up." Ben Graham offers another arresting analogy to illustrate this tendency:

> the market is not a *weighing machine,* on which the value of each issue is recorded by an exact and impersonal mechanism, in accordance with its specific qualities. Rather should we say that the market is a *voting machine*, whereon countless individuals register choices which are the product partly of reason and partly of emotion.

In the near term, stock prices oscillate around true worth, and at times the amplitude of divergence can be significant. In the longer term, however, the truth will out. As Buffett comments, "The market may ignore business success for a while, but eventually will confirm it."

Market efficiency, for value investors, is therefore a question of timing – although not agreeing that financial exchanges are invariably efficient in the short run, they generally accept that in the long run stock markets are indeed very effective "weighing machines." As pioneering fund manager John Bogle observed, "The fact is that when the perception – interim stock prices – vastly departs from the reality – intrinsic corporate values – the gap can only be reconciled in favor of reality." This is due to a simple and indisputable mathematical identity – over time, stockholders, in aggregate, can only earn what the underlying business earns. Animal spirits lack endurance – they may deflect prices from underlying value for a period of time, but ultimately the hard realities of earnings and dividends will determine the value of a business to its owners. Empirical evidence confirms the effectiveness of stock markets as a weighing machine over the longer term. As one report concludes, although year-to-year stock performance is heavily influenced by price movements:

For the seriously long-term investor, the value of a portfolio corresponds closely to the present value of dividends. The present value of the (eventual) capital appreciation dwindles greatly into insignificance.

BARGAIN HUNTING

Annual income twenty pounds, annual expenditure nineteen nineteen and six, result happiness. Annual income twenty pounds, annual expenditure twenty pounds ought and six, result misery.

—Charles Dickens, *David Copperfield*

Intelligent investors, then, look for stocks where the quoted price has for some reason uncoupled from any reasonable assessment of earnings potential. Value investing, at its simplest, is the act of getting more than is given – for a buyer of stocks, securing a stream of cash flows whose present value is expected to exceed the purchase price, for a seller of stocks, pocketing sale proceeds which exceed any reasonable estimate of future dividends. As Warren Buffett summarizes, value investors:

> search for discrepancies between the *value* of a business and the *price* of small pieces of that business in the market ... The investors simply focus on two variables: price and value.

It is on expected earnings and dividends, therefore, that the value investor concentrates, rather than short-term price fluctuations. The quoted price of a stock is useful only as a point of reference, in determining whether the market is offering substantially more or less than the estimated underlying value of the security. In explaining his investment philosophy to a colleague, Keynes remarked that:

> My purpose is to buy securities where I am satisfied as to assets and ultimate earning power and where the market price seems cheap in relation to these.

As Keynes emphasized, when ascertaining the underlying value of a stock, it is its "ultimate earning power" that is relevant. The "intrinsic" or "fundamental" value of a stock is simply the sum of expected cash flows from a given security, appropriately discounted for the effects of time. Other measures commonly thought to satisfy value investment precepts – such as low price-to-earnings ratios, low price-to-book value, and a high dividend yield – are, at best, tools for identifying possibly underpriced stocks. Ultimately, however, it is the expected earning power of a stock that counts.

The value investor, therefore, adopts a "bottom-up," rather than "top-down," investment style – that is, the investor scrutinizes *particular* stocks in an effort to determine whether there exists a discrepancy between the quoted price of the business and its assessed underlying value. Other factors – whether the stock price has trended up or down in recent times, what other stock markets are doing, whether a particular sector is "hot" at the moment – are of no interest to the intelligent investor. As renowned stock-picker and financier Sir John Templeton counseled, the disciplined investor should "buy value, not market trends or the economic outlook." The value investor focuses on specific stocks rather than the broader index, and remembers always that there is no such thing as an undifferentiated "stock market" – there is only a market for individual stocks.

EYES FORWARD

> *The future ain't what it used to be.*
>
> —Yogi Berra (attributed)

Humans are pattern-making animals, always seeking to impose order or a *raison d'être* where it does not necessarily exist. They discern faces in clouds and winning streaks in a coin toss, and three dots on a piece of paper will always resolve into a triangle. Likewise in the stock market, many game players believe that the trend is their friend – that what happened in the recent past is as good a guide as any as to what might happen in the future. As Keynes observed in one of his Chairman's speeches at a National Mutual annual meeting, "Speculative markets ... are governed ... by fear more than by forecast, by memories of last time and not by foreknowledge of next time." Speculators generally rely on *past* events – price momentum and perceived market trends – as buying or selling cues.

In contrast, value investors – those who scrutinize individual stocks rather than attempting to take the temperature of the market – focus only on the likely *future* income from a particular security. For these individuals, the investment decision is driven not by a mere expectation that prices will rise or fall over the short term, but rather by an assessment of whether stock prices appear cheap or expensive, based on an estimate of what earnings are likely to do in the long term. Intelligent investors concentrate on the business behind the stock, speculators on the stock price independent of the business. Practitioners of value investing always have intrinsic value as the bedrock of their decision-making – price merely offers a point of entry (or exit) to the investor, should it move far enough from the estimated underlying value of the security.

VIRTUE REWARDED

> *I am still convinced that one is doing a fundamentally sound thing, that is to say, backing intrinsic values, enormously in excess of the market price, which at some utterly unpredictable date will in due course bring the ship home.*
>
> —Keynes to the Managing Director of Provincial Insurance Company, April 10, 1940

Keynes, as one of his Bloomsbury contemporaries observed, "loved a bargain." Notwithstanding his growing wealth and generous financial support of the arts, he watched over his personal finances with surprisingly keen eyes. Keynes was not above haggling with tradesmen over a few pence, would buy large consignments of war-issue bully beef because it was only a penny a tin, and hosted dinner parties that were legendary for their frugality. Virginia Woolf noted that on one occasion Keynes served a miserly three grouse to his eleven guests – the visitors' "eyes gleamed as the bones went round," she later remarked with a regulation Bloomsbury barb. The Bloomsberries, grousing about the grouse, may have extracted a few sardonic laughs at Keynes' expense, but perhaps they missed a key point about the man. The remarkable fact was not that Keynes was a resolute bargain hunter despite his great wealth, but rather that the bulk of his riches were derived precisely *because* he was a bargain hunter.

In the final phase of his investment career, Keynes focused on identifying "stunners" – those stocks which offered "intrinsic values ... enormously in excess of market price." Although Keynes professed scant faith in the efficiency of financial exchanges at any given point in time, he did concede that, in the longer term, the stock market would recognize the value inherent in a security and reward performance. The intelligent investor, therefore, focuses on the *future earnings ability* of a *particular* stock, rather than being diverted by past trends in the market as a whole. Short-term price fluctuations, the excitement generated by an influx of animal spirits, stock market whims and fashions – all these are of absolutely no import to the discriminating investor. The only relevant factor is the disparity, if any, between price and the estimated intrinsic value of a stock.

Keynes' value investing discipline effectively shielded him from the assaults of animal spirits during the 1930s and 1940s. Unlike Newton, who during the South Sea insanity followed the crowd and neglected to flex his mental muscles in the field of finance, Keynes applied his own analysis rather than trying to anticipate the market. In a letter to Richard Kahn, a former pupil and Second Bursar at King's, Keynes summarized his value investing philosophy as follows:

> It is a much safer and easier way in the long run by which to make investment profits to buy £1 notes at 15*s.* than to sell £1 notes at 15*s.* in the hope of repurchasing them at 12*s.* 6*d*.

Or, rephrasing this maxim in decimal terms, we could say that it is preferable to buy one-dollar bills at seventy cents, rather than selling them at seventy cents in the hope of subsequently repurchasing the notes at fifty cents.

To return to the beauty contest analogy in *The General Theory,* a value investor – after proper reflection – will determine whom she or he thinks is the prettiest contender, rather than trying to second-guess the second-guesses of others. The intelligent investor has faith that, eventually, the most attractive contestant will ascend to the podium.

9.

SAFETY FIRST

THE FALL OF THE NOUS OF USSHER

I would rather be vaguely right, than precisely wrong.

—Keynes (attributed)

JAMES USSHER WAS A MAN of many talents – Archbishop of Armagh, Primate of All Ireland, Privy Councillor, and Vice-Provost of Dublin's Trinity College. But perhaps the Archbishop's greatest gift to posterity was his detailed study on the chronology of the Bible, undertaken in the mid-seventeenth century during the last decade of his life. By adding up the genealogies of Adam and his brood, and painstakingly cross-referencing these against other classical texts, Ussher deduced the exact date of Creation. The world, he declared, saw its first sunrise on Sunday, October 23, 4004 BC. Working from this absolute base, he could then calculate other key dates from Genesis – Adam and Eve, for example, were ejected from Paradise on Monday, November 10, 4004 BC, and Noah's Ark finally bumped into Mount Ararat on May 5, 2348 BC, a Wednesday.

Archbishop Ussher's ecclesiastical exactitude – subsequently modified by Isaac Newton in his own quest to fathom the secrets of the scriptures – is an object lesson in the perils of precision. Likewise, in the sphere of stock market investing, Keynes recognized that – due to unavoidable uncertainty surrounding future earnings – determining the intrinsic value of a stock was a necessarily fuzzy art. He had little time for the "brand of statistical alchemy" that many stock analysts brought to their calculations, in which the alleged value of a security was derived with pinpoint accuracy. Precision in stock valuation was nothing more than a consoling fiction, Keynes thought, perhaps designed to provide the illusion of certainty in an inherently unpredictable world.

Like Warren Buffett after him, Keynes rejected the application of a bogus precision when estimating the intrinsic value of a stock. He realized that not only does an overemphasis on quantitative factors downplay non-numerical elements that may impact on the value of a stock, but – due to uncertainty – any stock valuation must of necessity be inexact, lying at best within a range of possible values. The prudent investor, therefore, incorporates a wide margin of error into any assessment of the relative merits of a security. Inverting the mindset of the typical speculator, value investors focus as much on not losing money as on potential gains – they are concerned with the return *of* capital, not just the potential return *on* capital. In his effort to avoid what he called "stumers" – situations "where the fall in value is due not merely to fluctuations, but to an intrinsic loss of capital" – Keynes focused on a policy of "safety first", of ensuring that a protective buffer exists between a stock's price and its perceived underlying value.

OMISSION POSSIBLE

Life is the art of drawing sufficient conclusions from insufficient premises.

—Samuel Butler, *The Note-Books of Samuel Butler*

In 1922, while in Germany to advise on currency reform, Keynes found himself seated next to Max Planck at a dinner for Berlin's financial and academic elite. Planck, a recent Nobel Prize winner for his pioneering work in quantum physics, revealed to his dinner companion that – perhaps influenced by a Munich professor's rueful observation years earlier that in the field of physics "almost everything is discovered, and all that remains is to fill a few holes" – he had at one stage considered studying economics. Ultimately, however, Planck had declined the opportunity to join the ranks of the dismal scientists – economics, he had decided, was simply too difficult.

What Planck meant, Keynes later explained, was that economics was an "amalgam of logic and intuition," incapable of distillation into the flinty certainties of the physical sciences, and it was this lack of precision that made it "overwhelmingly difficult" for a man of Planck's rigorous and deductive disposition. Although Keynes' response to Planck's observation was not recorded, he no doubt would have congratulated the professor on his perspicacity. Keynes believed that, in a misguided effort to mimic the theoretical rigor of the physical sciences, classical economics clung too tightly to a "specious precision", at the expense of "concealed factors" that are not capable of quantification.

Friedrich von Hayek – Keynes' philosophical opposite in most other areas – shared these reservations. In his Nobel Prize lecture, Hayek noted that "in the study of such complex phenomena as the market ... [many factors] will hardly ever be fully known or measurable." Classical economists laboring under a "scientistic" attitude, Hayek observed, simply disregard those factors which "cannot be confirmed by quantitative evidence" and "they thereupon happily proceed on the fiction that the factors which they can measure are the only ones that are relevant." Keynes similarly deplored the "Ricardian vice" which he believed pervaded classical economic thought – the crystallization of all interrelationships and all activities into mathematical formulas, and the dismissal of qualitative elements as unworthy of analysis. "When statistics do not seem to make sense," he once remarked, "I find it is generally wiser to prefer sense to statistics!"

ORIGINS OF THE SPECIOUS

> *There are three kinds of lies: lies, damned lies and statistics.*
>
> —Mark Twain, *The Autobiography of Mark Twain*

Despite the fact that the only certainty about future returns from a security is their very uncertainty, a similar defect afflicts the stock market – analysts solemnly apply rigorous quantitative techniques to derive a valuation, down to the last cent, for a particular stock. Berkshire Hathaway's Charlie Munger has labeled this bias toward quantification, at the expense of qualitative factors, as the "man with a hammer" syndrome – "To the man with only a hammer," he observes, "every problem looks like a nail." Echoing Hayek's criticisms, Munger notes that:

> practically everybody (1) overweighs the stuff that can be numbered, because it yields to the statistical techniques they're taught in academia, and (2) doesn't mix in the hard-to-measure stuff that may be more important.

It appears that human psychology demands this spurious precision in an effort to mask the uncertainty inherent in any investment decision. As Fred Schwed observed in *Where Are the Customers' Yachts?*, his classic account of Wall Street's foibles:

> It seems that the immature mind has a regrettable tendency to believe, as actually true, that which it only hopes to be true. In this case, the notion that the financial future is not predictable is just

> too unpleasant to be given any room at all in the Wall Streeter's consciousness.

Keynes agreed that this sham exactitude was the stock market's equivalent of whistling in the dark, noting that "peace and comfort of mind require that we should hide from ourselves how little we foresee."

Elaborate quantitative analysis may also be an attempt to clothe mere hunches in a cloak of intellectual respectability. The economist Robert Shiller, author of the book *Irrational Exuberance*, remarks that sometimes:

> institutional investors do not feel that they have the authority to make trades in accordance with their own best judgments, which are often intuitive, that they must have reasons for what they do, reasons that could be justified to a committee.

Complex and comprehensive spreadsheets – calculating cash flows, risk-adjusting returns, deriving stock valuations with unimpeachable certitude – are often nothing more than an elaborate alibi, designed to confer a bogus authority to inherently uncertain subject matter.

GIRL IN THE GORILLA SUIT

> *Not everything that counts can be counted, and not everything that can be counted counts.*
>
> —Sign hung in Albert Einstein's Princeton study

The psychology experiment sometimes known as "the girl in the gorilla suit" illustrates how focusing too tightly on some factors can distort the bigger picture. In this experiment, subjects were shown a short video of two teams passing a basketball among themselves, and were asked to count the number of passes made by one of the teams. While team members are firing basketballs at each other, a woman in a gorilla suit lopes on to the court, stops, faces the camera and pounds her chest before moving off-screen. Around half of the participants in the exercise claimed not to have seen the apish apparition – they were simply too preoccupied with diligently counting the number of passes made by "their" team.

In a similar way, an excessive focus on quantitative data can warp stock valuations. As Ben Graham commented:

> the combination of precise formulas with highly imprecise assumptions can be used to establish, or rather to justify, practically any value one wishes ... in the stock market the more elaborate and abstruse the mathematics the more uncertain and speculative are the conclusions we draw therefrom.

Graham's own solution to this problem was not to reduce his reliance on quantitative factors, but rather to impose a more onerous test on potential acquisitions. In his book *The Intelligent Investor*, Graham suggested "readers limit themselves to issues selling not far above their tangible-asset value." Such a high hurdle would, he thought, ensure that investors secured a sufficient "margin of safety" in their stock purchases.

THE FEAR OF ALL SUMS

> *Charlie Munger: We have such a "fingers and toes" style around here. Warren often talks about these discounted cash flows, but I've never seen him do one ...*
> *Warren Buffett: That's true. It's sort of automatic. If you have to actually do it with pencil and paper, it's too close to think about. It ought to just kind of scream at you that you've got this huge margin of safety.*
>
> —Berkshire Hathaway annual meeting, 1996

In determining whether a stock displayed the necessary margin of safety – a sufficiently wide gap between assessed intrinsic value and quoted price – Ben Graham exhibited his own particular variant of the "man with a hammer" syndrome. His valuation approach was essentially a static one, concentrating mainly on the value of a company's physical assets. This technique might have been appropriate in the wake of the Great Depression – where stocks were sometimes offloaded at fire-sale prices and physical assets constituted the bulk of a firm's worth – but it is of limited practical value in today's world, where it is estimated that over 80 percent of the market value of companies in the Standard & Poor's 500 comprises intangible assets, such as brand names, patents and "human capital."

Keynes, like Warren Buffett after him, practiced a more dynamic valuation methodology – one focused on projected earnings accruing to a particular firm. The notional tool used in this type of analysis is the "dividend discount model". This model states that the intrinsic value of a given security is determined by the stream of its prospective dividend payments over time, discounted back to a present value. Warren Buffett highlighted the tasks required of an investor using this technique:

> If you buy a bond, you know exactly what's going to happen, assuming it's a good bond ... If it says 9 percent, you know what the coupons are going to be for maybe thirty years ... Now, when you buy a business, you're buying something with coupons on it, too, except, the only problem is, they don't print the amount. And it's my job to print in the amount on the coupon.

Unlike government or corporate bonds – which carry a known coupon and a predetermined maturity date – the expected income flow from a security cannot be determined with any degree of precision. Instead, the investor must refer to qualitative factors when determining the value of a stock. Warren Buffett provides an everyday analogy to describe the derivation of intrinsic value:

> It's exactly what I would do if I were going to buy a Ford dealership in Omaha – only with a few more zeros. If I were going to try and buy that business – let's say I weren't going to manage it – I'd try to figure out what sort of economics are attached to it: What's the competition like? What can the return on equity likely be over time? Is this the guy to run it? Is he going to be straight with me? It's the same thing with a public company. The only difference is that the numbers are bigger and you buy them in little pieces.

Ascertaining the intrinsic value of a stock is a necessarily inexact art – as Buffett observes, the underlying or fundamental value of a stock is "a number that is impossible to pinpoint but essential to estimate."

THE HALF-EMPTY GLASS

> *Fish see the bait, but not the hook; men see the profit, but not the peril.*
>
> —Chinese proverb

Intrinsic value, then, is a nebulous measure, existing at best within a range of possibilities. The importance of qualitative elements means that calculations of intrinsic value, properly done, cannot move beyond a fairly basic level of analysis – as Ben Graham observed, he had never "seen dependable calculations made about common-stock values ... that went beyond simple arithmetic or the most elementary algebra." The benefit of intrinsic value calculations lies as much in providing a checklist to ensure that the investor has turned his or her mind to all major factors potentially impacting the price of a security as in ascertaining an actual range of values. As Warren Buffett explains:

> Just as Justice Stewart found it impossible to formulate a test for obscenity but nevertheless asserted, "I know it when I see it," so also can investors – in an inexact but useful way – "see" the risks inherent in certain investments without reference to complex equations or price histories.

Compensating for this necessary imprecision is the concept of a margin of safety – a buffer, in Ben Graham's words, "for absorbing the effect of miscalculations or worse than average luck." Value investors, accepting the inexactness of intrinsic value measures, seek to identify those stand-out stocks that appear to display an undeniably large gap between underlying worth and quoted price. Although these "ultra-favourites" or "stunners," as Keynes called them, may not display a sharply defined intrinsic value, a sufficient margin of safety should nevertheless be evident. Ben Graham and his co-author David Dodd explained the concept in their book Security Analysis:

> To use a homely simile, it is quite possible to decide by inspection that a woman is old enough to vote without knowing her age or that a man is heavier than he should be without knowing his exact weight.

Value investing is, in essence, a "glass half-empty" rather than "glass half-full" approach – it focuses on downside risks rather than those on the upside. By selecting only those stocks that appear to be priced at a substantial discount to intrinsic worth, the investor seeks to ensure that there is a "floor" of underlying value that should support pricing over the longer term. The speculator, in contrast, is principally concerned not with the underlying earnings of a business but rather whether the stock can be offloaded at a higher price. As Fred Schwed observed:

> Speculation is an effort, probably unsuccessful, to turn a little money into a lot. Investment is an effort, which should be successful, to prevent a lot of money from becoming a little.

Keynes noted that for those seized by animal spirits, "the thought of ultimate loss ... is put aside as a healthy man puts aside the expectation of death." Value investors, on the other hand, focus heavily on downside risks before investing, by seeking to ensure a sufficient margin of safety exists in respect of any potential purchase.

PICK-A-NUMBER

> *Having a past actually counted against a company, for a past was a record and a record was a sign of a company's limitations... You had to show that you were the company not of the present but of the future.*
>
> —Michael Lewis on dot-coms, *The New New Thing*

Reviewing a journal article on statistical methods, Keynes recalled the mythical account of the seventy scholars asked to translate the Old Testament into Greek for inclusion in the Library of Alexandria:

> It will be remembered that the seventy translators were shut up in seventy separate rooms with the Hebrew text and brought out with them, when they emerged, seventy identical translations. Would the same miracle be vouchsafed if seventy [analysts] were shut up with the same statistical material?

Keynes had very little faith in the ability of purely quantitative methods to come up with meaningful estimates of intrinsic worth. Quoting the nineteenth-century journalist Walter Bagehot, he agreed that "there is no place where the calculations are so fine, or where they are employed on data so impalpable and so little 'immersed in matter'" as on the stock exchange. Consequently, there exists a very fragile foundation for the calculation of a stock's underlying value, and there may be widely divergent opinions on the worth of a security.

Recognizing that, due to both uncertainty and the presence of qualitative factors, a range of possibilities was the best that could be expected when assessing the underlying worth of a stock, Keynes adopted a "safety first" policy that sought to identify those stocks trading at a substantial discount to even low-range estimated intrinsic value. He realized that "the amount of the risk to any investor principally depends, in fact, upon the degree of ignorance respecting the circumstances and prospects of the investment he is considering." In other words, as uncertainty surrounding expected future cash flows increases, so too does the "fuzziness" of intrinsic value measures – consequently, a greater margin of safety is required.

Keynes observed that some stocks are more amenable to a tighter calculation of intrinsic value than others, and are therefore more compatible with a safety first policy. In *The General Theory* he noted that:

> there are many individual investments of which the prospective yield is legitimately dominated by the returns of the comparatively near future ... In the case of ... public utilities [for example], a substantial proportion of the prospective yield is practically guaranteed by monopoly privileges coupled with the right to charge such rates as will provide a certain stipulated margin.

Warren Buffett repeated the point in a letter to Berkshire Hathaway stockholders, in which he commented that "the more uncertain the future of a business, the more possibility there is that the calculation will be wildly off-base."

A BIRD IN THE HAND

Unquestionably, the really right policy would be to aim at as high an income as possible, and not to trouble too much about capital valuations.

—Keynes to the Chief Officer of National Mutual, January 19, 1939

The tenets of value investing – which demand a wide margin of safety in respect of securities acquired – will naturally bias investors toward stocks with a relatively stable and sustainable earnings profile. Serial acquirers – corporate Pacmen with the capacity to hide earnings performance behind the latest acquisition – are of little interest to the value investor, nor are stocks offering the promise of "blue sky" returns at some indefinite point in the future. Warren Buffett explained his preference for those stocks sometimes dismissively labeled as "boring" by citing Berkshire Hathaway's investment in Californian chocolate manufacturer See's Candies in the early 1970s:

> See's was . . . then annually earning about $4 million pre-tax while utilizing only $8 million of net tangible assets. Moreover, the company had a huge asset that did not appear on its balance sheet: a broad and durable competitive advantage that gave it significant pricing power. That strength was virtually certain to give See's major gains in earnings over time. Better yet, these would materialize with only minor amounts of incremental investment. In other words, See's could be expected to gush cash for decades to come.

In an undergraduate essay on the British philosopher and statesman Edmund Burke, Keynes noted in passing that:

> Our power of prediction is so slight, our knowledge of remote consequences so uncertain, that it is seldom wise to sacrifice a present benefit for a doubtful advantage in the future.

Keynes' observation was a rather baroque restatement of the proverb "a bird in the hand is worth two in the bush." In the stock market arena, too, Keynes eventually adhered to this principle – "ultimate earning power," not the vague promise of riches in some undefined future period, was fundamental in determining the worth of a stock.

Warren Buffett similarly insists on "demonstrated consistent earning power" before he commits capital to a particular security. It is earnings – not market capitalization, revenue growth, or the novelty of an industry – that will ultimately determine the value of a company, and therefore its stock price. A business that draws in $50 billion of revenue but, because of poor margins, ekes out the profit of a market stall is worth very little to the rational investor. Similarly, companies lacking defensible barriers to competitive entry may not have sustainable long-term earnings, and therefore will be of little interest to the disciplined stock-picker.

MAINTAINING AN EDGE

> *I am generally trying to look a long way ahead and am prepared to ignore immediate fluctuations, if I am satisfied that the assets and earning power are there . . . If I succeed in this, I shall simultaneously have achieved safety-first and capital profits.*
>
> —Keynes to the Chairman of Provincial Insurance Company, February 6, 1942

Unlike many of his peers, Keynes did not harbor a secret desire to make economics as inflexible and austere as Euclidean geometry. "Economics is essentially a moral science and not a natural science," he maintained, "that is to say, it employs introspection and judgments of value." Similarly, Keynes disclaimed the need for – or possibility of – precision in the stock market domain. The unavoidable presence of uncertainty – the fact that, in regard to the future, "we simply do not know" – combined with the existence of factors which impact on a stock's value but cannot be quantified, means that the task of ascertaining the underlying value of a stock is a necessarily inexact art.

Accepting that intrinsic value can, at best, lie somewhere within a range of values, Keynes developed a safety-first policy in respect of his stock acquisitions. Considering both quantitative and non-numerical factors, he assessed a firm's "assets and ultimate earning power" and compared the implied value of the entire company against the market's asking price for part-shares in that business. By "backing intrinsic values … enormously in excess of the market price," Keynes was confident that he would achieve his stated objectives of both "safety first" and, eventually, capital gains.

Warren Buffett's investment policy is very similar to that of Keynes. He accepts that "valuing a business is part art and part science" and therefore advocates a margin of safety – a financial shock absorber – to compensate for this lack of precision:

> You also have to have the knowledge to enable you to make a very general estimate about the value of the underlying businesses. But you do not cut it close. That is what Ben Graham meant by having a margin of safety. You don't try and buy businesses worth $83 million for $80 million. You leave yourself an enormous margin. When you build a bridge, you insist it can carry 30,000 pounds, but you only drive 10,000 pound trucks across it. And that same principle works in investing.

Exactitude in the stock market arena is a fiction – because of uncertainty, no one can value a security precisely. The best response to this uncertainty, Keynes and Buffett argue, is to ensure a wide buffer exists between perceived value and quoted price. Eventually, as the stock market reasserts its function as a weighing machine, this margin of safety should be converted into an investor's margin of gain.

10.

LEANING INTO THE WIND

APPLES FOR PEANUTS

Necessity never made a good bargain.

—Benjamin Franklin, *Poor Richard's Almanack*

IN MARCH 1918 THE GERMAN army – its eastern forces loosed after a treaty with newly Bolshevik Russia – gambled on a massive assault on the Western Front before the resources of that awakened giant, America, could be fully deployed. Ground which had been so expensively purchased in previous years – thousands of men killed for every few hundred yards of swampy, torn earth – now yielded itself freely to the Central Powers, and in just a few days *Sturmtruppen* were encamped on the outskirts of Paris. From these redoubts the Germans employed a fearsome new weapon, gigantic guns capable of hurling payloads high into the stratosphere and more than 80 miles distant – well within range of the center of Paris.

The success of the German Spring Offensive and the destruction inflicted by the unseen "Big Berthas" generated enormous panic in the French capital. Thousands of Parisians streamed west from the city, but battling against this current of people was Maynard Keynes. He had heard from his friend and former lover, the painter Duncan Grant, that the private collection of Edgar Degas was to be auctioned in Paris in late March. Grant and the Bloomsbury set urged Keynes to deploy his government connections to obtain funds to bid for these artworks. By proposing an ingenious scheme to offset any purchases against existing French debts to Britain, and arguing that "fine specimens of Masters" would be a much better bet than financially distressed French Treasury bills, Keynes extracted more than half a million francs from the Exchequer. Keynes was so taken with the operation, in fact, that not only did he secure the means for the National Gallery to bid for the Degas collection, but he also decided to attend the auction in person.

As Big Bertha periodically belched forth another shell, Keynes and the Director of the National Gallery – who, in true cloak-and-dagger style, had shaved off his moustache and donned spectacles to avoid detection by art dealers and the press – purchased twenty-seven paintings and drawings from the collection. Prices were so depressed by the fear and uncertainty caused by the encircling enemy that – despite the quantity and quality of the acquisitions, including works by Gauguin, Manet, and Delacroix – a quarter of the Treasury's grant remained unspent. Not only did this coup earn the grudging respect of the Bloomsberries – one offered the backhanded compliment that "your existence at the Treasury is at last justified" – but it also proved a personal boon for Keynes. Failing to convince his covert traveling partner of the merits of Cezanne, Keynes bought the post-impressionist's celebrated still life, *Apples*, on his own account for the ridiculously small sum of £327.

It would take more than a decade before Keynes applied the lessons learned in the Paris showroom to the domain of stock market investing. Abandoning the bandwagon-jumping approach of "credit cycling" during the turmoil of the late 1920s and early 1930s, he turned instead to a diametrically opposed investment style – one that focused on acquiring a handful of stocks at prices offering a substantial discount to expected future earnings potential, regardless of the whims and fashions of the market. After many successes and reversals, Keynes had eventually discerned that the stock market could, on occasion, be myopic, excessively optimistic or pessimistic, flighty, or propelled by informational cascades. It was at these times that the value investor's contrarian mantra that "one should be greedy when others are fearful, and fearful when others are greedy" came into its own.

FASHION VICTIM

> *What is pronounced strengthens itself.*
> *What is not pronounced tends to nonexistence.*
> —Czeslaw Milosz, "Reading the Japanese Poet Issa"

Belying his impeccable Establishment credentials, Keynes was the scion of a long line of religious dissenters on both sides of his family. This ancestral trait of nonconformism, in Maynard's case, seemed to extend well beyond matters of the spirit – in everyday life he delighted in paradoxes, opposed accepted wisdom, and, as the social reformer Beatrice Webb observed, disliked "all the common-or-garden thoughts and emotions that bind men together in bundles." A policy of "leaning into the wind," as he sometimes called contrarian investing, was ideally suited to Keynes' temperament – not only did it allow him to indulge the "perverse, Puckish" side of his nature, but his natural inclination to run counter to conventional thinking also offered the tangible satisfaction of financial gain.

Keynes rejected the more strident claims of efficient markets proponents, believing instead that, on occasions, a preponderance of "game players" over "serious-minded individuals" could produce a sustained divergence between quoted prices and underlying stock value. Like many other spheres of activity, stocks could be subject to the whims of fashion, caught up in the roiling currents of informational cascades where rising prices produce rising prices or falling prices engender further declines. Fred Schwed applied a characteristically cynical interpretation to this phenomenon:

> Those classes of investments considered "best" change from period to period. The pathetic fallacy is that what are thought to be the best are in truth only the most popular – the most active, the most talked of, the most boosted, and consequently, the highest in price at that time. It is very much a matter of fashion, like Eugenie hats or waxed mustaches.

The stock exchange is, at times, patently *not* the exemplar of efficiency that orthodox theorists claim it to be. Notwithstanding its proclaimed role as a machine to crystallize expected future cash flows, the market on occasions succumbs to "the fundamental fundamental" – in an exuberant bull market, more willing buyers than sellers; in a despondent bear market, more willing sellers than buyers.

The ripples from these waves of optimism or pessimism affect even those stocks initially untouched by investor irrationality, as capital is channeled into "hot" stocks and away from others. As Ben Graham commented in *The Intelligent Investor*:

> The market is fond of making mountains out of molehills and exaggerating ordinary vicissitudes into major setbacks. Even a mere lack of interest or enthusiasm may impel a price decline to absurdly low levels.

This displacement effect was particularly evident, for example, in the dying months of the twentieth century, when the rush to "new economy" shares created a two-speed market – on many exchanges the "TMT" trinity of telecommunications, media, and technology stocks broadly doubled in only a couple of years, while the derisively labeled "old economy" stocks languished out of the limelight.

THE PERILS OF POPULARITY

> *If fifty million people say a foolish thing, it is still a foolish thing.*
>
> —Anatole France (attributed)

Even Berkshire Hathaway, that beacon of levelheadedness and contrarian values, appears itself to have been the periodic plaything of fashion. As Charlie Munger – who jokingly describes himself as "assistant cult leader" at the company – comments, "what we have created at Berkshire … is, to some extent, a cult … [and] I think it's had effects on the stock prices of … Berkshire." Some individuals have been known to acquire one or two Berkshire Hathaway shares merely for the right to attend the stockholders' annual meeting and sit at the feet of Buffett and Munger. Conversely, in the last years of the 1990s – when Buffett was dismissed by many as a ponderous investment dinosaur doomed to extinction in the brave new world of dot-coms – Berkshire's stock became less modish and, in consequence, suffered a rare period of underperformance relative to the market.

Berkshire Hathaway's experience is a case study in the life cycle of stocks-as-fashion accessories. A stock is first picked up by the cognoscenti because of some particular attribute – in Berkshire's case, the immoderate success of its value investing approach. As enthusiasm for the stock percolates through the wider market and investors jump on the brimming bandwagon, prices may overshoot any reasonable estimate of intrinsic value. And when the stock inevitably falls out of favor – as happened with Berkshire Hathaway in the late 1990s, when investors deserted old economy stocks for the blue sky of early internet plays – prices "overcorrect" on the downside.

A similar process – although far more exaggerated – was seen on Wall Street in the late 1920s and early 1930s. When Edgar Lawrence Smith published his seminal book in 1924, his key conclusion – that through the operation of retained earnings, stocks were effectively "compound interest machines" – launched the cult of the common stock. American equities – which had previously displayed no strong price trend, either up or down, over time – enjoyed annual growth rates of around 30 percent in the three calendar years following publication of Lawrence's study. Light-headed at these dizzying altitudes, the market subsequently overbalanced and crashed. As Warren Buffett remarked, "What the few bought for the right reason in 1925, the many bought for the wrong reason in 1929." Stocks are contrary creatures – when they are most despised they promise the greatest rewards, and when most loved they present the greatest potential hazard.

BACKING THE RIGHT HORSE

A difference of opinion is what makes horse racing and missionaries.

—Will Rogers, *The Autobiography of Will Rogers*

The model that perhaps most resembles that of the stock market is the humble racetrack. At the races, bettors compete against other bettors, the odds on horses constantly moving to reflect the perceived favorites. Additionally, horses are handicapped with varying weights in an attempt to level the playing field – horses with a good win record will carry heavier weights than less successful nags. The stock market displays a very similar dynamic – investors compete with each other, buying and selling stocks based on their apparent prospects, and stocks perceived to have more potential are "handicapped" by higher price-to-earnings multiples than those securities deemed to be less promising.

In an ideal world – the world posited by efficient markets diehards – prices generated on the stock exchange by buyers and sellers will reflect the relative merits, in terms of earnings potential, of a security, so that each share is as good a bet as the other. In an interview with *Outstanding Investor Digest*, Berkshire Hathaway's Charlie Munger expanded on this point:

> Everybody goes [to the racetrack] and bets and the odds change based on what's bet. That's what happens in the stock market. Any damn fool can see that a horse carrying a light weight with a wonderful win rate and a good post position ... is way more likely to win than a horse with a terrible record and extra weight and so on ... But if you look at the odds, the bad horse pays 100 to 1, whereas the good horse pays 3 to 2. Then it's not clear which is statistically the best bet ... The prices have changed in such a way that it's very hard to beat the system.

In a broadly efficient stock market – as with a correctly priced horse race – it is indeed extremely difficult to beat the system. The key to success in both these arenas, therefore, is to identify the radically mispriced bet – the horse or stock that offers good odds *and* has a strong chance of performing.

Increasing the difficulty of the investor's or bettor's task is the fact that "the house" – the stock exchange for the investor, the racing authority for the bettor – retains a percentage of each wager laid. Although the stock market's take is not nearly as large as that of the racetrack, and historically the stock market pie generally grows larger over time, the principle still holds – successful investors and bettors must not only out-bet the rest of the market, but also receive a margin large enough to compensate for the transaction costs incurred in laying the wager. Success on the stock market, as Charlie Munger reminds us, requires the individual "to understand the odds and have the discipline to bet only when the odds are in your favor."

FEAR FACTOR

Our distrust is very expensive.

—Ralph Waldo Emerson, *Nature*

Stock markets, although bedevilled by uncertainty, exist *because* of uncertainty. As John Kenneth Galbraith noted:

> Were it possible for anyone to know with precision and certainty what was going to happen to ... the prices of stocks and bonds, the one so blessed would not give or sell his information to others; instead, he would use it himself, and in a world of uncertainty his monopoly of the certain would be supremely profitable. Soon he would be in possession of all fungible assets, while all contending with such knowledge would succumb.

Simply stated, financial markets exist because certainty does not – markets are as much an exchange of opinions as an exchange of capital and securities.

Keynes realized that radically mispriced stock market bets are most abundant when there exists great uncertainty and, in consequence, widely divergent opinions about the value of a stock. As he explained to a colleague, "The art of investing, if there is such an art, is that of taking advantage of the consequences of a mistaken opinion which is widespread." In making this observation, Keynes echoed an insight of Frank Knight, a University of Chicago academic. Knight noted that there were two types of uncertainty – measurable probability, which he labeled "risk," and unquantifiable ambiguity, which was true uncertainty. "Risk" can be assigned a probability value – such as the 50 percent chance of throwing heads in a coin toss or the one-in-six prospect of rolling a particular number on a dice – whereas "uncertainty" is utterly unmeasurable.

In the free enterprise system, Knight asserted, only true uncertainty – "ignorance of the future," as he described it – can consistently create potentially profitable situations, as quantifiable risk should, in theory, already be factored into the pricing of an asset.

Those investors wishing to profit from the stock market, therefore, are those who embrace uncertainty. As Keynes noted, "It is because particular individuals, fortunate in situation or in abilities, are able to take advantage of uncertainty and ignorance ... that great inequalities of wealth come about." Uncertainty, in respect of stocks, may be attributable to ambiguity about the business prospects of a particular company, more generalized misgivings about the state of the stock market or the broader economy, or some combination of these factors. The value investor – fortified by a perceived margin of safety operating to his or her advantage – exploits uncertainty, rather than being cowed by it.

GROCERIES, NOT PERFUME

People always clap for the wrong things.

—Holden Caulfield, in J.D. Salinger's *The Catcher In The Rye*

The stock market – the apotheosis of the free market system – frequently confounds a fundamental tenet of economics. When the price of a stock goes up, demand for that stock tends to *increase*, often merely because the price has risen. Similarly, when the price of a stock falls, demand for the stock often subsides. In so doing, the market betrays its true nature – it is under the influence of "game players," stock market participants concerned primarily with short-term price movements rather than longer-term earnings profiles. Warren Buffett provides a contrarian reality check on this behavior:

> many [investors who expect to be net buyers of investments throughout their lifetimes] illogically become euphoric when stock prices rise and unhappy when they fall. They show no such confusion in their reaction to food prices: Knowing they are forever going to be buyers of food, they welcome falling prices and deplore price increases. (It's the seller of food who doesn't like declining prices.)

If stocks are perceived as dividend-paying vehicles, then the investor is not afraid of corrections – indeed, a decline in exchange value should be viewed favorably, as it allows the investor to get more "quality for price" in terms of income as a proportion of initial outlay. Only speculators – those who perceive stocks as trading assets – will ordinarily view stock price declines negatively. The rules of price theory and utility maximization deem that the rational individual will be disposed to buy more of something the cheaper it becomes. With stocks, price and demand are often correlated because the "return" most people consider is capital gain, and as the market declines the prospect of trading profits falls commensurately.

It was on this psychological quirk – the tendency for the market to be influenced by short-term price patterns – that Keynes based much of his investment philosophy. Discussing the disposition of the American stock market, he commented to a colleague that:

> Very few American investors buy any stock for the sake of something which is going to happen more than six months hence, even though its probability is exceedingly high; and it is out of taking advantage of this psychological peculiarity that most money is made.

Value investors focus on long-term earnings, not short-term price cascades. As Ben Graham noted, intelligent investors buy their stocks as they buy their groceries, not as they buy their perfume – *value* is the key consideration, not the short-winded enthusiasms of the rabble.

KISSING TOADS

> *If you can keep your head when all about you are losing theirs …*
> then maybe they know something you don't.
>
> —Market maxim

Adhering to a policy of value investing – basing investment decisions on an analysis of intrinsic value rather than price momentum – means that value investors are often on the "other side" of the market. A contrarian policy is not, however, simply one of automatically opposing the mob, reflexively zigging when others zag. The practice of blind contrarianism is just as dangerous as bandwagon-jumping investing styles – like momentum investing, it dispenses with fundamental value analysis in favor of market timing and requires the speculator to divine something as fickle as mob psychology. As always, the investment decision should be motivated by an assessment of the estimated intrinsic value of a particular stock relative to its quoted price, not by market sentiment one way or another.

One of Keynes' first recorded contrarian forays, for example, foundered on the rocks of reality. In late July 1914, on the same day that the Austro-Hungarian Empire declared war on Serbia and markets recoiled at the prospect of a pan-European conflict, Keynes bought a parcel of mining and transport shares. In effect, he wagered that hostilities would remain localized – "The odds appear to me *slightly* against Russia and Germany joining in," he wrote to his father on the day of purchase – and that stock prices would, in consequence, rebound. Keynes' optimism proved to be woefully misplaced – two days later, Russia ordered the general mobilization of its army, and the Germans then formally declared war on Russia. The dominoes were toppling and the Great War would embroil a large proportion of the developed world. In the arrogant flush of youth, Keynes had forgotten that markets, on many occasions, successfully execute their idealized role as an "intelligent multitude."

Ironically, the world's most successful investment institution, Berkshire Hathaway, draws its name from a failed business investment – a "turnaround" that failed to turn. In the mid-1960s, when Warren Buffett acquired the company, Berkshire Hathaway seemed to satisfy many of the rule-of-thumb measures used in identifying potentially underpriced opportunities – low price-to-book value, low price-to- earnings ratio, and so on. But the market, in this case, had been correct in marking down the price of Berkshire stock. As Buffett recounts:

> [Berkshire Hathaway] made over half of the men's suit linings in the United States. If you wore a men's suit, chances were that it had a Hathaway lining. And we made them during World War II, when customers couldn't get their linings from other people. Sears Roebuck voted us "Supplier of the Year." They were wild about us. The thing was, they wouldn't give us another half a cent a yard because nobody had ever gone into a men's clothing store and asked for a pin striped suit with a Hathaway lining.

Berkshire lacked pricing power – its products were mere commodities and therefore subject to fierce competitive pressure. Two decades after his acquisition of the company, Buffett was forced to shut down the last of Berkshire Hathaway's textile operations.

MONOPOLY MONEY

> *Better a diamond with a flaw than a pebble without.*
>
> —Confucius

The early misadventures of Berkshire Hathaway illustrate a broader lesson learned by both Keynes and Buffett – the importance of acquiring interests in businesses possessing a sustainable competitive advantage, or commercial "moats" as Buffett describes them. Berkshire Hathaway's original business, textile manufacturing, was a commodity-type industry requiring high capital expenditure and delivering generally poor returns. Better long-term business investment prospects, Buffett discovered, lay in those companies possessing sturdy barriers to competition, such as unique franchises, settled oligopolies, or well-known brand names.

Buffett emphasizes "the importance of being in businesses where tailwinds prevail rather than headwinds" – the ultimate investment opportunity presents itself, he advises, "when a great company gets into temporary trouble." In this respect, Buffett departs from the practice of his mentor, Ben Graham. Graham believed in buying average businesses at cheap prices – he would build a widely diversified portfolio of those stocks meeting his simple but rigorous quantitative measures, in the expectation that a sufficient number of these businesses would surmount their vicissitudes and eventually increase in price. Buffett's investment criteria, in contrast, focuses more on qualitative factors – he looks for "great companies with dominant positions, whose franchise is hard to duplicate and has tremendous staying power or some permanence to it."

In this emphasis on quality – buying companies with defensible moats at fair prices – Buffett reflects the approach of Keynes. In an early magazine article, Keynes endorsed the virtues of "blue chips":

> It is generally a good rule for an investor, having settled on the class of security he prefers – . . . bank shares or oil shares, or investment trusts, or industrials, or debentures, preferred or ordinary, whatever it may be – to buy only the best within that category.

Most alleged "turnaround" plays offer a very flimsy margin of safety to the value investor – predictions of future income based on optimistic "blue sky" projections will always be highly speculative. For the long-term investor, quality companies are a much better bet. As Charlie Munger explains:

> Over the long term, it's hard for a stock to earn a much better return than the business which underlies it earns. If the business earns 6 percent on capital over 40 years and you hold it for ... 40 years, you're not going to make much different than a 6 percent return – even if you originally buy it at a huge discount. Conversely, if a business earns 18 percent on capital over 20 or 30 years, even if you pay an expensive looking price, you'll end up with a fine result.

A long-term investor, harnessing the enormous cumulative power of compounding, will reap a greater return from steadily increasing earnings than from a one-off bargain purchase.

MINORITY REPORT

> *Many shall be restored that are now fallen and many shall fall that are now in honor.*
>
> —Horace, *Ars Poetica*

Empirical evidence, when viewed over a longer time horizon, tends to support a policy of contrarian investing. Numerous studies show that in the long term "value" stocks outperform "growth" stocks – that is, securities with relatively low price-to-earnings multiples and price-to-book value ratios, and relatively high dividend yields, have provided better returns to the investor over time. Even Professor Eugene Fama, the University of

Chicago academic known as "the father of efficient markets theory," has himself become something of a heretic among orthodox financial theorists with his findings that value stocks tend to produce higher returns than growth stocks in most of the world's major exchanges.

However, in the short term a "momentum effect" – where prices follow a trend for a sustained period of time – is discernible in many financial asset markets. This tendency for rising prices to continue rising and falling prices to keep falling – a further affront to the efficient markets hypothesis – has been ascribed to a number of factors, including investor inertia in adjusting to new information, the "window-dressing" of portfolios at financial period end by professional managers, and the slower rhythms of the underlying business cycle. More recent explanations for stock market momentum include the increasing returns to scale accruing to large technology companies as they benefit from network effects, with success breeding more success as the moat around the business widens with each new customer.

Generally, the momentum effect is strongest in the short term while over the longer term the phenomenon of "reversion to the mean" predominates. The economist Robert Shiller, citing one study, notes that:

> ten-year real returns on the Standard & Poor's index have been substantially negatively correlated with price-earnings ratios at the beginning of the period.

What this means in practice, Shiller explains in simple terms, is that "when the market gets high, it has tended to come down." The behavioral economists Richard Thaler and Werner De Bondt, examining a broad sample of underperforming stocks, found that "a strategy of buying extreme losers over [the preceding two to five years] ... earns significant excess returns over later years," with prior "losers" outperforming prior "winners" by around 8 percent per year. Reversion to the mean – the tendency for stocks that have beaten the index in the short term to underperform the market in the longer term, and vice versa – can be viewed as a visible manifestation of the stock market reasserting itself as a weighing machine rather than a voting machine by eventually reining in pricing overshoots.

BUY ON THE SOUND OF CANNONS

> *Even outside the field of finance, Americans are apt to be unduly interested in discovering what average opinion believes average opinion to be; and this national weakness finds its nemesis in the stock market.*
>
> —Keynes, *The General Theory*

One of Keynes' colleagues at the Provincial Insurance Company recalled an occasion when a member of the Investment Committee suggested buying Indian government bonds. "By all means," Keynes responded, "but timing is important. Wait 'til a Viceroy has been assassinated!" Maynard Keynes realized that it was periods of uncertainty that produced the conditions necessary for "stunners" to emerge. A rather extreme example of this tendency – and one that gives credence to the charge of economics as the dismal science – was the experience of Keynes' protégé, the Italian economist Piero Sraffa. According to one story circulating within Cambridge, Sraffa – who was in possession of a substantial family inheritance – waited patiently for "the one perfect investment." Shortly after the bombing of Hiroshima and Nagasaki by the Allies, he invested heavily in Japanese government bonds – and subsequently reaped a fortune in Japan's post-War "miracle years."

Keynes himself exploited the tremendous uncertainty and fear created during the Great Depression to effect his greatest contrarian triumph. In late 1933, when shell-shocked American investors flinched at FDR's robust anticorporate rhetoric, Keynes started buying preferred shares of utility companies, reasoning that they were "now hopelessly out of fashion with American investors and heavily depressed below their real value." Despite fears that Roosevelt would nationalize electricity utilities, Keynes acquired significant shareholdings in the belief that:

> some of the American preferred stocks offer today one of those outstanding opportunities which occasionally occur of buying cheap into what is for the time being an irrationally unfashionable market.

In the following year alone, Keynes' net worth would almost triple, largely on the back of his plunge on Wall Street.

Similarly, Warren Buffett achieved perhaps his most spectacular contrarian coup during another deep stock market slump. In 1974, when many pundits were proclaiming that "the Death of Equities" was imminent, Buffett acquired a large stake in *The Washington Post*. As Buffett explains, due to the overwhelming pessimism oppressing the market, the company was undervalued on any reasonable measure:

> In '74 you could have bought the *Washington Post* when the whole company was valued at $80 million. Now at that time the company was debt free, it owned *The Washington Post* newspaper, it owned *Newsweek*, it owned the CBS stations in Washington, D.C. and Jacksonville, Florida, the ABC station in Miami, the CBS station in Hartford/New Haven, a half interest in 800,000 acres of timberland in Canada, plus a 200,000-ton-a-year mill up there, a third of the *International Herald Tribune*, and probably some other things I forgot. If you asked any one of thousands of investment analysts or media specialists about how much those properties were worth, they would have said, if they added them up, they would have come up with $400, $500, $600 million.

The radically mispriced bet – in this case, one evidenced by even a fairly basic sum-of-parts calculation of key assets – is most often thrown up amidst conditions of great uncertainty. As Buffett continually reminds his disciples, "Fear is the foe of the faddist, but the friend of the fundamentalist." Bolstered by a perceived margin of safety, the value investor exploits this uncertainty, rather than being intimidated by it.

LONESOME IN THE CROWD

> *[Stock market investing] is the one sphere of life and activity where victory, security, and success is always to the minority and never to the majority. When you find anyone agreeing with you, change your mind. When I can persuade the Board of my Insurance Company to buy a share, that, I am learning from experience, is the right moment for selling it.*
>
> —Keynes to a fellow stock investor, September 28, 1937

Keynes was a defiant individualist and very diffident team player. He once joked that his chief hobby was "fluttering dovecotes, particularly in the City," and the man sometimes seemed constitutionally incapable of finding accord with the majority. In the closing stages of World War II, during loan negotiations with the United States, Keynes' frustration with consensus-building excited some of his finest invective. He called Leo Crowley, the American administrator of the Lend-Lease scheme, a "Tammany Polonius" whose "ear [was] so near the ground that he was out of range of persons speaking from an erect position," and observed for good measure that the unfortunately florid Crowley had a face like "the buttocks of a baboon." Of Marriner Eccles, chairman of the Federal Reserve and a key member of the American negotiating team, he commented: "No wonder that man is a Mormon. No single woman could stand him." James Meade, later a winner of the Nobel Prize in economics, unsurprisingly described the fiercely independent Keynes as "a menace in international negotiations."

Similarly, Keynes – the instinctive contrarian – was uncomfortable with an investment-by-committee approach. In an ostensibly contrite letter to a fellow member on the Eton finances committee, he explained:

> My central principle of investment is to go contrary to general opinion, on the ground that, if everyone agreed about its merits, the investment is inevitably too dear and therefore unattractive. Now obviously I can't have it both ways – the whole point of the investment is that most people disagree with it. So, if others concerned don't feel enough confidence to give me a run, it is in the nature of the case that I must retire from unequal combat.

Keynes discerned that one cannot consistently outperform the crowd when one is part of it – as Ben Graham advised, sustained success on the stock market can only be achieved by following an investment policy that is "(1) inherently sound and promising, and (2) not popular on Wall Street." Unlike some of his investment committee colleagues, Keynes realized that value investing is a matter of facts, not fashion – ascribing an intelligence to the masses, as if knowledge could be weighed rather than evaluated, is a sure path to underperformance.

Value investors are almost by definition contrarians – an underpriced stock implies that the broader market has not recognised, or at least has underestimated, the earnings potential of that security. Contrarian investing, however, demands more effort than a mere reflexive opposition to prevailing market sentiment – one needs to be a good swimmer to go against the flow. Stock market "dogs" can bite, and the value investor must be satisfied, after his or her own independent analysis, that the underlying company possesses a sustainable earnings flow. Warren Buffett distinguishes "extraordinary business franchises with a localized excisable cancer" from turnarounds "in which the managers expect – and need – to pull off a corporate Pygmalion." Value investors – realizing that, all other things being equal, a fall in stock prices will allow them to acquire more earnings for a given outlay – are not upset by a decline in prices, provided that the earnings prospects of the underlying business remain substantially unchanged. The intelligent investor understands that lack of present popularity does not necessarily translate into lack of future profitability.

11.

BEING QUIET

HOMAGE TO CATATONIA

Wisely and slow; they stumble that run fast.

—Shakespeare, *Romeo and Juliet*

KING'S COLLEGE, KEYNES' ALMA mater, is famed for its medieval chapel, considered one of the finest examples of late Gothic architecture anywhere in the world. Declared the most beautiful church in England by Henry James, it was immortalized by William Wordsworth as a "glorious work of fine intelligence ... Where light and shade repose, where music dwells." It was into this place of otherworldly beauty, built by Henry VI to redound the glory of God, that Maynard Keynes strode one day in the mid-1930s with a very specific task in hand. He surveyed the chapel's lofty pillars and vaulted ceilings, but not, on this occasion at least, for their aesthetic charms. Rather, Keynes – mathematician that he originally was – proceeded with a rough reckoning of the cubic capacity of the building. His purpose was to determine whether the chapel could accommodate a large and imminent shipment of grain from South America.

Owing to one of his more flamboyant commodity plays, Keynes was about to be encumbered with the equivalent of a month's supply of wheat for the whole of the United Kingdom. Rather than pay the difference between the spot price of wheat and the contract price – the conventional method for settling a futures contract – Keynes elected to back his judgment and take physical delivery of the grain, confident that the market rate would eventually rise beyond his contracted price. In a rare victory for aesthetics over commerce, Keynes' impertinent scheme to convert the King's College chapel into a granary was averted – apparently the building was simply not big enough to store the consignment. Instead, Keynes stalled by objecting to the quality of the cargo, complaining that the wheat contained more than the permitted number of weevils per cubic foot. By the time the grain was cleaned, the market price had risen such that the wily economist eventually made money on the contract.

Keynes' preposterous plan to turn the hallowed chapel into one of history's more elegant barns was emblematic not only of his transformation from callow aesthete to hardheaded money-man, but also the change in his investment philosophy from momentum investing to one of "faithfulness" in respect of a handful of "pets". As an early value investor, Keynes believed that "'Be Quiet' is our best motto" – short-term price fluctuations could be ignored as mere "noise" and the disciplined investor should patiently wait for the market to reassert itself as a weighing machine rather than a voting machine. The only rational response to irrational mob behavior, he determined, was to let the game players have the short term to themselves, while Keynes instead practiced a policy of "steadiness" in respect of his select portfolio of shares.

This buy-and-hold strategy was not only the natural complement to an investment philosophy that assessed stocks on the basis of future income streams, but it also offered long-term investors the not inconsiderable advantages of significantly lower transaction costs, and allowed them to reap the enormous power of compound interest.

WHIRLPOOLS OF SPECULATION

> *Speculators may do no harm as bubbles on a steady stream of enterprise. But the position is serious when enterprise becomes the bubble on a whirlpool of speculation. When the capital development of a country becomes a by-product of the activities of a casino, the job is likely to be ill-done.*
>
> —Keynes, *The General Theory*

Teddy Roosevelt, the trust-busting American President of the early twentieth century, once asserted that "there is no moral difference between gambling at cards or in lotteries or on the race track and gambling in the stock market." Keynes disagreed with this assessment – he thought that gambling on the stock market was far more deleterious to a nation's health than the innocent pleasures of the track or the gambling den. In an appearance before a Royal Commission in 1932, he argued that "it is much better that gambling should be associated with frivolous matters of no great significance rather than be bound up with the industry and trade of the country." Keynes believed that racecourses and the like were a relatively harmless safety valve for the speculative urge. "Industrial betting" on stock exchanges, on the other hand, could lead to "the whole of [a nation's] industry becoming a mere by-product of a casino."

Keynes contrasted the socially destructive effects of stock market game players with those of speculators in the commodity and currency markets. This latter class of speculator, Keynes asserted, provided "a useful, indeed almost an essential, service" by providing certainty in otherwise risky situations:

> Where risk is unavoidably present, it is much better that it should be carried by those who are qualified or are desirous to bear it, than by traders, who have neither the qualification nor the desire to do so, and whose minds it distracts from their own business.

In contrast, the "proper social purpose" of the stock market was, as Keynes explained, "to direct new investment into the most profitable channels in terms of future yield." The price performance of a stock will influence not only the ability of the underlying company to raise capital on the equity market, but will also affect the company's borrowing capacity, its ability to make acquisitions, and the types of strategies it seeks to implement. A fundamental tenet of discriminating capitalism is that the stock market should reward those businesses that are the most successful. Success in the capitalist system is defined in brutally reductionist terms – the ability to earn sustainable profits over time.

Only "enterprise" investing, where the investment decision is informed by an estimate of the total prospective yield of a security, facilitates this social purpose. Stock market speculation – which, as Ben Graham remarked, "is largely a matter of A trying to decide what B, C, and D are likely to think – with B, C, and D trying to do the same" – merely serves to distort capital flows, by potentially diverting capital and kudos away from performing businesses. As Keynes noted in *The General Theory*, "The social object of skilled investment should be to defeat the dark forces of time and ignorance which envelop our future." In Keynes' perfect world, the stock market would be populated by individuals buying securities "for keeps", based on "long-term forecasts of the probable yield of an investment over its whole life" – not by trigger-fingered game players attempting to anticipate short-term swings in mass psychology.

TIME ON YOUR SIDE

> *Foul-cankering rust the hidden treasure frets,*
> *But gold that's put to use more gold begets.*
>
> —Shakespeare, *Venus and Adonis*

Keynes had a happy ability to produce economic theories that conformed to his own personal beliefs. One of the chief conclusions of *The General Theory* – that moribund economies could be kick-started by government spending – coincided perfectly with his view that money was meant to be spent, not hoarded. Keynes' advocacy of "a somewhat comprehensive socialization of investment" reflected his faith in state-appointed mandarins to, in certain circumstances, do a better job than the mobbish market. And his views on speculation in the stock market – as opposed to the currency and commodity markets – were in tune with his later incarnation as a value investor, while still allowing Keynes an occasional flirtation with the commodity and foreign exchange pits.

Both during his life and posthumously, Keynes weathered many attacks accusing him of a form of intellectual contortionism: essentially, molding his theories so that they satisfied his personal predilections. In his defense, however, socially responsible stock market investing – a policy of "steadfast holding" of stocks acquired on the basis of anticipated yield – also happened to be most congenial to the creation of wealth in the long term. A long investment horizon not only allows investors to look beyond the distractions of constantly fluctuating prices, but also shields them from the erosion of capital inevitably produced by transaction costs inherent in trading.

Perhaps more importantly, a philosophy of "being quiet" – of limiting activity in the market only to those occasions when quoted prices appear to stray far from intrinsic value – allows the investor to reap the tremendous power of compound interest. Compound interest works like a kind of financial snowball – if income from an asset is reinvested, this income will in turn earn income, and the original capital contribution grows at a geometric rate. The "rule of 72" neatly illustrates the exponential increases available from compounding. Dividing the number 72 by the yield earned on an investment provides a close approximation of the amount of time required for a sum of income-earning capital to double in value – for example, a sum yielding 6 percent return per year, if re-invested, will double in twelve years, and an asset with a 9 percent per annum yield will double in value in only eight years.

The intelligent investor, recruiting time as his ally in the value-creation process, relies on what Keynes called the "powerful operation of compound interest" rather than the vagaries of the market. For the buy-and-hold value investor, it is time in the market – rather than market timing – that is important.

ERRORS OF COMMISSION

> *Stockjobber: a low wretch who gets money by buying and selling shares in the funds.*
>
> —Samuel Johnson, *A Dictionary of the English Language*

Even from a relatively early age, Keynes viewed brokers and investment managers in a generally unfavorable light. In *Indian Currency and Finance*, his first book, Keynes asked rhetorically:

> how long will it be found necessary to pay City men so entirely out of proportion to what other servants of society commonly receive for performing social services not less useful or difficult?

Later in life, he advised his nephew – just setting out in the world of investment – not to take any notice of brokers' suggestions. Keynes hinted that a type of reverse Darwinism operated among the broking fraternity, a survival of the dimmest. "After all," he reasoned with his young charge, "one would expect brokers to be wrong. If, in addition to their other inside advantages, they were capable of good advice, clearly they would have retired a long time ago with a large fortune."

The Berkshire Hathaway duo share Keynes' distaste for the financial advisory profession. Warren Buffett drolly notes that "Wall Street is the only place that people ride to work in a Rolls Royce to get advice from those who take the subway," and Charlie Munger has drafted in Keynes to support his argument:

> I join John Maynard Keynes in characterizing investment management as a low calling. Because most of it is just shifting around a perpetual universe of common stocks. The people doing it just cancel each other out.

As Gordon Gekko, that famous demystifier of Wall Street, explained, stock market investing, in aggregate, is "a zero sum game – somebody wins, somebody loses." Interposing another level of intermediaries must, therefore, necessarily reduce the aggregate returns available to investors as a whole.

But brokers and investment managers exert a far more insidious effect on stock market game players. Like sharks, appropriately, brokers and other financial intermediaries require constant movement in order to survive. The interests of investors and brokers are poorly aligned – brokers are geared toward "churning" trades, thereby maximizing commissions, at the expense of the investor. Not only do brokers encourage excessive trading – "Never ask a barber if you need a haircut," Warren Buffett quips – but commissions, bid-ask spreads, and other agency costs can seriously erode the capital base of an active investor.

CAPITAL PUNISHMENT

> *The avoidance of taxes is the only intellectual pursuit that still carries any reward.*
>
> —Keynes (attributed)

Brokers' charges and other transaction costs do, however, possess one positive attribute – they may act as something of a brake on excessive trading, encouraging stock market players to think twice before buying and selling, thereby sparing them from a potentially more punitive cost. The various forms of "capital gains tax" – a levy imposed on profits realized on the sale of assets, including stocks – are not in fact taxes on capital gains; rather, they are a *transaction* tax. An investor holding a stock that has improved in price merely incurs a *nominal* tax liability in respect of his gains – only when the security is sold will the tax liability crystallize.

Buy-and-hold investors sometimes receive concessions on "long- term capital gains" – the tax rate may, for example, be lower for investments held for more than a year. In addition to this explicit reduction in the tax rate, deferring a tax liability can – due to the power of compounding – have significant positive effects on the after-tax value of an investor's portfolio. An active market player who turns his portfolio over each year will incur an annual tax liability. The buy-and-hold investor, on the other hand, only incurs a *theoretical* tax liability for as long as he holds the stocks, and therefore still has his "before-tax" gains working for him – in effect, the investor receives an interest-free loan from the tax office. Due to the exponential effects of compounding, the buy-and-hold investor will – all other things being equal – record a significantly larger after-tax return.

Warren Buffett and Charlie Munger are particularly fierce critics of the "self-inflicted wounds" sustained from excessive market activity. Buffett cautions that a "hyperactive stock market is the pickpocket of enterprise," and Charlie Munger commends a policy of minimizing "frictional costs":

> There are *huge* advantages for an individual to get into a position where you make a few great investments and just sit back and wait: You're paying less to brokers. You're listening to less nonsense. And if it works, the governmental tax system gives you an extra 1, 2 or 3 percentage points per annum compounded.

As Buffett noted in a letter to Berkshire stockholders, "For investors as a whole, returns decrease as motion increases."

TO HAVE AND TO HOLD

> *I believe now that successful investment depends on ... [among other things] a steadfast holding of ... fairly large units through thick and thin, perhaps for several years.*
>
> —Keynes to the King's College Estates Committee, May 8, 1938

Keynes, better than most, understood the fleeting but intense satisfactions of the successful speculator. Writing in *The General Theory* with the guilty knowledge of the poacher-turned-gamekeeper, he observed that "human nature desires quick results ... and remoter gains are discounted by the average man at a very high rate." It was upon this psychological peculiarity – now pathologized as the condition of "hyperbolic discounting" by the behavioral finance fraternity – that Keynes laid the foundation for his tremendous stock market success in the latter part of his investment career. Not only was a long-term horizon consistent with an investment policy based on realizing the latent potential of underpriced stocks, but this "steadiness" also protected the investor from transaction costs that can seriously erode the capital of the active investor.

In *The General Theory* Keynes suggested that compelling stock market participants to adopt a long view would cure them of the malaise of short-termism and hyperactivity. "The introduction of a substantial government transfer tax on all transactions," he mused, "might ... [mitigate] the predominance of speculation over enterprise." This idea was later taken up by Warren Buffett, who argued that a 100 percent tax should be applied to profits made on stocks held for less than a year. Buffett's refusal to effect stock splits on Berkshire paper – the company has the highest priced stock on the New York Stock Exchange – is his own way of attempting to curtail the liquidity of, and therefore the speculative pressure on, Berkshire securities.

In considering the merits of a long-term approach to stock market investments, Keynes opined that:

> to make the purchase of an investment permanent and indissoluble, like marriage, except by reason of death or other grave cause, might be a useful remedy for our contemporary evils. For this would force the investor to direct his mind to the long-term prospects and to those only.

For Keynes at least, the marriage metaphor was apt. He had evolved from a type of financial philanderer – engaging in the monetary equivalent of one-night stands on the foreign exchange and commodities markets – to a more steadfast individual, remaining loyal to his select group of stock market "pets."

Warren Buffett also adopts a matrimonial analogy when discussing investment strategy, calling his stock market approach "our 'til-death-do-us-part policy" and remarking on Berkshire's "determination to have and to hold." Jesse Livermore, a famous stock trader and market bear in the early part of the last century, once likened Wall Street to a "giant whorehouse" where brokers pimped their stocks to the average Joe. Extending this admittedly crude metaphor, it might be said that Keynes – the reformed sinner, the speculator who eventually embraced the buy-and-hold approach – perhaps wanted to make honest women out of his stocks, seeking a faithful and fruitful relationship with his select handful of "stunners." As Buffett reminded his stockholder congregation in one of his missives, investors are not rewarded for activity – they are rewarded for being right.

12.

EGGS IN ONE BASKET

A FUGITIVE FROM THE LAW OF AVERAGES

Too much of a good thing can be wonderful.

—Mae West, in *My Little Chickadee*

KEYNES' PATERNAL GRANDFATHER, LIKE his illustrious descendant, was adept at turning a profit. Exploiting England's enduring obsession with gardening, he accrued a small fortune from his flower-growing business, making his first financial killing during the "dahlia craze" of the 1840s. Keynes senior was a shrewd businessman who resolutely focused on only the most lucrative flower strains – first dahlias, later roses and carnations – rather than, in the words of one gardening magazine of the time, "embark[ing] money and strength in dubious enterprises." Like his forebear, Maynard Keynes also believed that investing heavily in a few "pets" would typically deliver much better returns than an indiscriminate policy of diversification.

Keynes was repeatedly reprimanded for making big plays on only a small number of stocks. In response to criticism from a colleague at Provincial for purchasing "a large and exceptional unit" in a shipping company, Keynes bristled:

> Sorry to have gone too large in Elder Dempster … I was … suffering from my chronic delusion that one good share is safer than ten bad ones, and I am always forgetting that hardly anyone else shares this particular delusion. The price has, I think, now gone up by about *6d*, so you can get rid of any surplus without loss that you would like to.

In his indomitably contrarian way, Keynes rejected the orthodox view that an optimal stock portfolio is one that is widely diversified. Conventional financial theory decrees that markets are efficient – that is, all stocks are correctly valued and one stock is just as likely as another to rise or fall in price in response to unknowable future events. Building on this assumption, accepted wisdom argues that it is better to hold a large number of stocks so as to minimize the impact of random underperformance by any particular share. Diversification is the stock market application of the maxim "don't put all your eggs in one basket."

Keynes, like Warren Buffett after him, did not agree with this approach – he thought that a patient and informed investor could select a small group of "ultra-favourites" having "prospects of rising enormously more than an index of market leaders." When these few "stunners" – or, as Buffett calls them, "superstars" and "grand-slam home runs" – are periodically thrown up by the market, intelligent investors should not be afraid to invest a relatively large proportion of their funds in these stocks.

Accordingly, in the latter half of his investment career Keynes maintained an extremely compact stock portfolio, with over half the value of his total stockholding represented by the shares of only a few firms. For his faith in portfolio concentration, Keynes was rewarded with an investment performance far superior – albeit more volatile – than that of the broader market.

BASKET CASE

I puts it all away, some here, some there, and none too much anywheres, by reason of suspicion.

—Long John Silver, in Robert Louis Stevenson's *Treasure Island*

Portfolio diversification is essentially a defensive strategy – by spreading funds between a large number of stocks, the extent to which poorly performing shares affect overall portfolio value is reduced. Further, the greater the diversification within a stock portfolio – that is, the more representative it becomes of the market as a whole – the lesser the risk of underperforming *relative to the market*. This outcome is important to both orthodox theorists and the average investor. Conventional financial wisdom defines "risk" as the *volatility* of a portfolio relative to the broader market, and therefore asserts that a diversified portfolio must, by definition, be less "risky" than a more compact suite of stocks. The average investor, too, is generally risk averse and accepts that lower potential portfolio gains is the price to be paid for reducing the risk of potential losses.

Although Keynes himself was never satisfied with a merely middling result, he did concede that a policy of "scattering one's investments over as many fields as possible might be the wisest plan" for an individual with no special knowledge of the stock market. Warren Buffett repeated the point in a shareholder letter:

> Diversification serves as protection against ignorance. If you want to make sure that nothing bad happens to you relative to the market, you should own everything. There's nothing wrong with that. It's a perfectly sound approach for somebody who doesn't know how to analyze businesses.

Keynes thought that, for an individual who cannot or will not rigorously apply the precepts of value investing, "it ought to be considered as imprudent for such a man to make his own investments as to be his own doctor or lawyer."

For these investors, index funds – investment vehicles that mimic broad market performance by building an appropriately weighted portfolio of stocks – offer low-cost exposure to the stock market. As Buffett explained to Berkshire Hathaway shareholders, an unsophisticated investor seeking "to be a long-term owner of industry" should:

> both own a large number of equities and space out his purchases. By periodically investing in an index fund, for example, the know-nothing investor can actually out-perform most investment professionals. Paradoxically, when "dumb" money acknowledges its limitations, it ceases to be dumb.

Moreover, an investor committing a fixed sum to an index fund at regular intervals – a practice known as "dollar cost averaging" – will automatically counteract the excesses of Mr. Market. When Mr. Market is in his manic phase – bidding up prices way above their fundamental value – the investor will buy fewer shares per investment contribution, due to the higher cost per share. Conversely, when Mr. Market is in a down period – with shares sinking far below fundamental value – the investor will purchase more shares for the same outlay. Dollar cost averaging is a simple, self-regulating contrarian strategy, absolving the unsophisticated investor from any misguided efforts to second-guess the market.

IF YOU CAN BEAT THEM, DON'T JOIN THEM

> *A man must consider what a rich realm he abdicates when he becomes a conformist.*
>
> —Ralph Waldo Emerson, *Journals*

The price of joining the crowd, however, is that one will never stand out from it – diversification limits volatility not only on the downside, but on the upside also. For an individual with a good understanding of the market, Keynes believed that a diversified stock portfolio made no sense whatsoever. He thought that those investors who could properly analyze stocks should focus only on potential "stunners" and – when the market occasionally presents them to the investing public – buy them in meaningful quantities.

Toward the end of his investment career, Keynes concluded that:

> it is out of these big units of the small number of securities about which one feels absolutely happy that all one's profits are made ... Out of the ordinary mixed bag of investments nobody ever makes anything.

Similarly, the Berkshire Hathaway duo endorse the idea of "loading up" on "grand-slam home runs" – Charlie Munger commends an investment policy of "making a few great investments and sitting back," and Buffett advises that "the important thing is that when you do find [a 'superstar'] where you really do know what you are doing, you must buy in quantity." To borrow one of Buffett's aphorisms, "If something is not worth doing at all, it's not worth doing well": the impact of scoring a "home run" will be diluted if the stock constitutes only a small portion of total portfolio value.

Portfolio concentration can produce better results than diversification due to a number of factors, including lower transaction costs – broker commissions proportionately decrease as deal size increases – and potentially lower administration costs. But perhaps the most compelling argument for portfolio concentration by informed investors is the simple logic expressed in one of Warren Buffett's shareholder letters:

> I cannot understand why an [educated] investor ... elects to put money into a business that is his 20th favorite rather than simply

> adding that money to his top choices – the businesses he understands best and that present the least risk, along with the greatest profit potential.

The same impulse that propels stock market speculation also motivates the drive toward diversification – the desire to be part of the crowd. As the financier Gerald Loeb recognized, a widely diversified portfolio "is an admission of not knowing what to do and an effort to strike an average" – for those investors who believe that they can in fact rank stocks, a policy of portfolio *concentration* is preferable.

KEEPING IT SIMPLE

> *The art of being wise is the art of knowing what to overlook.*
>
> —William James, *The Principles of Psychology*

Diversification is the tribute paid by investors to uncertainty. In what may well be the world's first pro-diversification tract, the Book of Ecclesiastes counsels the reader to:

> Send your grain across the seas, and in time you will get a return. Divide your merchandise among seven ventures, eight maybe, since you do not know what calamities may occur on earth.

This biblical injunction to go forth and diversify reflects the conventional reaction to uncertainty – moderate risks by diluting them as much as practicable. Diversification is, in reality, more a strategy of risk *dispersion* than risk reduction.

Keynes' response to uncertainty and risk in the share market was radically different to the prevailing wisdom – as he explained in a letter to one of his business associates:

> my theory of risk is that it is better to take a substantial holding of what one believes shows evidence of not being risky rather than scatter holdings in fields where one has not the same assurance.

To ascertain which stocks "show evidence of not being risky," the value investor searches for those securities that exhibit a sufficiently large margin of safety – that is, those stocks with a substantial gap between estimated intrinsic value and the quoted price.

In undertaking this analysis, the intelligent investor will necessarily focus only on those businesses he or she understands. Keynes noted that he would prefer "one investment about which I had sufficient information to form a judgment to ten securities about which I know little or nothing." His contention was that intelligent, informed investors will reduce their downside risk by scrutinizing only those sectors within their "circle of competence" – to use Buffett's phrase – and then only investing in those stocks which exhibit a satisfactory margin of safety. Like Socrates, intelligent investors are wise because they recognize the bounds of their knowledge.

SEARCHING FOR HOLES IN THE BASKETS

> *Put all your eggs in the one basket and – WATCH THAT BASKET.*
>
> —Mark Twain, *Pudd'nhead Wilson*

Paradoxically, diversification – like all forms of insurance – can actually encourage riskier behavior. Just as those with flood insurance may be tempted to build their houses closer to the water, or motorists wearing seatbelts may become more aggressive drivers, so, too, highly diversified investors may similarly feel that they can afford to have a flutter on a speculative stock play if there is relatively little at stake – as the economist-stockbroker David Ricardo rationalized, "I play for small stakes, and therefore if I'm a loser I have little to regret." Or, to quote Bob Dylan, a more modern authority on this phenomenon, "When you got nothing, you got nothing to lose."

In contrast to the diversified stockholder, the focus investor will ordinarily demand a significant margin of comfort prior to allocating substantial funds to a single stock. Fear of loss can concentrate the mind wonderfully, and the investor staking a large proportion of his or her total funds on only one security is more likely to rigorously scrutinize this potential investment. As Buffett summarizes, a policy of portfolio concentration should serve to increase "both the intensity with which an investor thinks about a business and the comfort-level he must feel with its economic characteristics before buying into it."

Focusing on only a handful of stocks should not, therefore, increase portfolio "risk," at least as it is defined by the layperson – that is, the possibility of incurring financial loss. The intelligent investor will only select those stocks that exhibit the largest shortfall between quoted price and perceived underlying value – that is, those securities that are likely to provide the greatest margin of safety against financial loss in the long term. Although a compact suite of stocks will be undeniably more volatile than a diversified holding, short-term price fluctuations are of little concern to a long-term holder of stocks who focuses on income rather than capital appreciation. Indeed, value investors favor those stocks that display the potential for extreme volatility – the difference is that these investors expect predominantly *upside* volatility. Risk, for value investors, is not a four-letter word – it is embraced and addressed proactively, not defensively.

WAITING FOR A FAT PITCH

I call investing the greatest business in the world because you never have to swing. You stand at the plate, the pitcher throws you General Motors at 47! US Steel at 39! and nobody calls a strike on you. There's no

> *penalty except opportunity lost. All day you wait for the pitch you like; then when the fielders are asleep, you step up and hit it.*
>
> —Warren Buffett, quoted in *Forbes* magazine

A policy of portfolio diversification is the logical outcome of a belief in efficient markets. As Keynes noted, it is "false to believe that one form of investment involves taking a view and that another does not. Every investment means committing oneself to one particular side of the market." A strategy of extreme diversification is, at its core, a concession by the investor that stock-picking is futile for that particular individual – that, indeed, one stock is as good as another. It is a candid admission that the market knows more than that person.

Keynes rejected the notion that markets always priced securities correctly based on publicly available information and that, therefore, it was pointless to search for potential stunners. His view was much more pragmatic, and was grounded in his experience as an investor and financial theorist: Keynes believed that financial exchanges – although perhaps *usually* efficient – were not *always* efficient. On occasions, the stock market generates prices that veer radically from underlying value – Mr. Market is perhaps in the throes of a particularly acute bipolar episode – and it is at these times that the intelligent investor should buy in quantity.

The poet Paul Valery once asked Albert Einstein if he kept a notebook to record his ideas – Einstein is said to have replied, "Oh, that's not necessary – it's so seldom I have one." Similarly, opportunities to buy quality stocks at a material discount to fundamental value are infrequent. As stock investor and author Philip Fisher commented:

> practical investors usually learn their problem is finding enough outstanding investments, rather than choosing among too many ... Usually a very long list of securities is not a sign of the brilliant investor, but of one who is unsure of himself.

Agreeing that "ultra-favourites" are usually thin on the ground, Keynes noted that "there are seldom more than two or three enterprises at any given time in which I personally feel myself entitled to put *full* confidence."

When the market does offer a security at a substantial discount to its intrinsic worth the investor should, therefore, acquire meaningful amounts of that stock. Charlie Munger opts for a metaphor close to his heart when explaining Berkshire Hathaway's policy of "loading up" on mispriced bets:

> Playing poker in the Army and as a young lawyer honed my business skills. What you have to learn is to fold early when the odds are against you, or if you have a big edge, back it heavily because you don't get a big edge often. Opportunity comes, but it doesn't come often, so seize it when it does come.

Good investment opportunities are too scarce to be parsimonious with, Buffett often reminds his acolytes – when a stunner presents itself, the value investor should not be afraid to back his or her judgment with relatively large capital outlays.

CROSSING THE JORDANS

> *You won't improve results by pulling out the flowers and watering the weeds.*
>
> —Peter Lynch, *One Up on Wall Street*

For an investor who – like Keynes and Buffett – adopts a buy-and-hold policy in respect of stocks, portfolio concentration is something that tends to happen naturally over time. Inevitably, some stocks within a portfolio will perform better than others and these "stunners" will come to constitute a large proportion of total value. A policy of portfolio concentration cautions against an instinctive desire to "re-balance" holdings just because an investor's stock market investments are dominated by a few companies.

Buffett illustrates this point with an analogy. If an investor were to purchase a 20 percent interest in the future earnings of a number of promising basketball players, those who graduate to the NBA would eventually represent the bulk of the investor's royalty stream. Buffett says that:

> To suggest that this investor should sell off portions of his most successful investments simply because they have come to dominate his portfolio is akin to suggesting that the Bulls trade Michael Jordan because he has become so important to the team.

Buffett cautions against selling off one's "superstars" for the rather perverse reason that they have become too successful. The decision to sell or hold a security should be based solely on an assessment of the stock's expected future yield relative to its current quoted price, rather than any measure of past performance. Insights from the field of behavioral finance confirm that investors have a tendency to sell assets that have increased in price while holding on to those that have fallen. This preference for selling the plums while keeping the lemons – known as the "disposition effect" – is doubly irrational given short-term pricing momentum often observed in the stock market, where rising stocks tend to keep rising in the near term.

EGGS IN A COUPLE OF BASKETS

> *Half of [my speculative positions] go up and half of them go down when the news is bad, and vice versa when the news is good; so I have what is called a "well-balanced position"*
>
> —Keynes to his mother, September 2, 1922

During his interview for a director's seat at National Mutual, Keynes ventured the opinion that "the right investment policy for [the Society] would be to hold one security only and change it every week at the board meeting." This rather hyperbolic remark was, no doubt, designed to dislodge the old guard from their stubborn attachment to a passive and property-oriented investment style. But although it was an ambit claim – intended to startle the frock-coated gents out of their comfortable complacency – it did reflect, to a large extent, Keynes' faith in "focus investing."

However, for all his enthusiasm for a compact portfolio, even Keynes conceded that the principle of concentration "ought not to be carried too far." Keynes accepted that the maintenance of "a balanced investment position" justified a certain degree of diversification within any stock holding. He defined a "balanced position" as one in which there were:

> a variety of risks in spite of individual holdings being large, and if possible opposed risks (e.g. a holding of gold shares amongst other equities, since they are likely to move in opposite directions when there are general fluctuations).

A portfolio of stocks with opposed risk characteristics will generally serve to offset, at least in part, the effect of unforeseen and unpredictable shocks to any particular security.

Additionally, investors may obtain some of the benefits of diversification, while still maintaining a focused portfolio, by spreading their capital between different asset classes – by holding not only stocks but also, for example, investments in property or bonds. Although Keynes' wealth was particularly concentrated in the stock market – he never owned a house or any other form of real property, and by the time of his death his securities portfolio represented over 80 percent of the total assessed value of his assets – most other investors display a preference for considerably less reliance on just one asset class. "Sell down to your sleeping point," the American financier J. Pierpont Morgan reportedly advised a friend whose slumber was being compromised due to worries about his stock portfolio. Similarly, most value investors may elect to adopt a slightly more wide-ranging investment approach than that of Keynes.

LOADING UP

> *To suppose that safety-first consists in having a small gamble in a large number of different directions ... as compared with a substantial stake in a company where one's information is adequate, strikes me as a travesty of investment policy.*
>
> —Keynes to the Chairman of Provincial Insurance Company, February 6, 1942

Compact portfolio construction emphasizes the *quality* of stocks rather than the quantity of stocks. For those investors who believe they know something of the market, or at least certain sectors within the market, it makes sense to focus on what Keynes called the "ultra-favourites." This handful of stocks – Keynes never prescribed an exact number, Buffett in one communiqué suggested "five to ten sensibly-priced companies" – will absorb the bulk of investible funds. Intelligent investors – because they know the companies they are analyzing and because their comfort levels will need to be high to justify such relatively large outlays – will satisfy themselves, after diligent analysis, that the investment is not too risky. They will not merely cast their money on a wide range of stocks about which they know very little, relying on a belief in the efficiency of markets to absolve them from any need to carefully analyze the underlying companies.

Focus investing, then, refers not just to the maintenance of a targeted portfolio of stocks, but also to the limited pool of stocks evaluated (those within an investor's "circle of competence"), and the laser-like intensity with which those stocks are assessed. The intelligent investor will not reflexively spread his or her funds across the universe of investment opportunities, for, as Keynes noted:

> To carry one's eggs in a great number of baskets, without having time or opportunity to discover how many have holes in the bottom, is the surest way of increasing risk and loss.

Contrary to conventional financial wisdom, Keynes argues that a focused portfolio should be *less* risky than a diversified portfolio, as investors will restrict their analysis to those stocks within their circle of competence and will also demand a wide margin of comfort prior to allocating a substantial proportion of total funds to a single stock.

It is ironic that in the high temple of capitalism, Adam Smith's commandment to specialize has been so comprehensively ignored. Dismissing the dogma of diversification, Keynes noted in a letter to the Chairman of the Provincial Insurance Company that:

> As time goes on I get more and more convinced that the right method in investment is to put fairly large sums into enterprises which one thinks one knows something about and in the management of which one thoroughly believes. It is a mistake to think that one limits one's risk by spreading too much between enterprises about which one knows little and has no reason for special confidence.

The level of investment risk in respect of a particular stock, Keynes emphasized, was commensurate with the level of ignorance and uncertainty surrounding that security. Value investing inverts the risk-return trade-off suggested in orthodox texts – those stocks offering the greatest apparent margin of safety, and therefore by definition the least downside risk, also potentially offer the greatest returns. By "loading up" only in respect of "stunners", as Keynes suggested, investors should both reduce the riskiness of their portfolio *and* give themselves the best chance of outperformance relative to the broader market.

13.

A SENSE OF PROPORTION

THE STOCK MARKET STOIC

> *Of all existing things some are in our power, and others are not in our power ... Let him then who wishes to be free not wish for anything or avoid anything that depends on others; or else he is bound to be a slave.*
>
> —Epictetus, *The Handbook*

MAYNARD KEYNES GRANTED ONLY conditional assent to Saint Timothy's belief that the love of money was the root of all evil. True, he had little time for the "strenuous purposeful moneymakers" motivated by "the love of money as a possession," but he also agreed with Samuel Johnson that there are few ways in which a man can be more innocently employed than in getting money. Keynes observed in *The General Theory* that:

> dangerous human proclivities can be canalized into comparatively harmless channels by the existence of opportunities for money-making and private wealth, which, if they cannot be satisfied in this way, may find their outlet in cruelty, the reckless pursuit of personal power and authority, and other forms of

> self-aggrandizement. It is better that a man should tyrannize over his bank balance than over his fellow-citizens.

In any case, those touched with "the moneymaking passion" were, as Keynes conceded, a necessary evil – it would be in the wake of these men, impelled by their striving after profit, that the rest of mankind would be dragged to the promised land of "economic bliss" and material abundance.

Keynes, in contrast to the energetic worshippers of Mammon, professed a much more utilitarian conception of money. As he coolly commented to his friend Duncan Grant, who was "very much enraged" to have received mere cash as a birthday gift, "The thing is good as a means and absolutely unimportant in itself." Later, in *A Tract on Monetary Reform*, he would return to the theme of money as a simple expedient:

> It is not easy, it seems, for men to apprehend that their money is a mere intermediary, without significance in itself, which flows from one hand to another, is received and is dispensed, and disappears when its work is done from the sum of a nation's wealth.

Moneymaking, Keynes thought, should be accorded its proper place – as an amusement, an intellectual game, a means to secure the good things in life.

Keynes' pragmatic attitude conferred on him a hardy resistance to the assaults of animal spirits, and engendered a more clear-sighted approach to stock market investing. After the false starts of his early investment career, Keynes realized that enduring success in the stock market accrued to those who exploited mob behavior rather than those who participated in it, and that a businesslike approach to investment decisions was infinitely preferable to blindly following the crowd. Keynes' lesson from the 1920s was that financial exchanges were inherently unpredictable, at least in the short term. Intelligent investors, then, accept that they cannot control the market's behavior and instead focus on controlling their own behavior – what is required, as Warren Buffett would later affirm, is "a sound intellectual framework for making decisions and the ability to keep emotions from corroding that framework."

DON'T JUST DO SOMETHING, STAND THERE ...

> *Investing should be more like watching paint dry or watching grass grow. If you want excitement, take $800 and go to Las Vegas.*
>
> —Paul Samuelson (attributed)

Keynes was not unaware of the tribute exacted by stock trading. In one biographical sketch, he described the German representatives at the Paris Peace Conference as a "sad lot with drawn, dejected faces and tired staring eyes, like men who had been hammered on the Stock Exchange." At first blush, this seems a curiously inappropriate simile – comparing the representatives of a vanquished nation to victims of a mere financial defeat – but the memoir was written in the summer of 1931, in the trough of the Great Depression and with the death of a former student still fresh in Keynes' mind. Sidney Russell Cooke, a fellow director at National Mutual and a "brilliant and engaging personality" in Keynes' estimation, took his own life the previous year as a result of losses on the stock exchange. Reversals in the world of money could, as Keynes discovered, claim a heavy toll on those weakened by the contagion of animal spirits.

In the subsequent calm, after he had restored his fortune on the back of value investing principles, Keynes concluded that the intelligent investor needed "as much equanimity and patience" as possible to withstand the periodic incursions of animal spirits and the distractions of fluctuating prices. Market liquidity and its concomitant, constant price quotation, is a double-edged sword – it enables investors to easily enter and exit the market, and thereby makes them "much more willing to run a risk," as Keynes noted, but minute-by-minute changes in stock prices can also foster a short-term mindset among stock market players. Keynes cautioned that:

> One must not allow one's attitude to securities which have a daily market quotation to be disturbed by this fact or lose one's sense of proportion. Some Bursars will buy without a tremor unquoted and unmarketable investments in real estate which, if they had a selling quotation for immediate cash available at each Audit, would turn their hair gray.

The intelligent investor, Keynes asserted, maintains "a sense of proportion" by accepting that for sustained periods a stock's price may split from its underlying value. The investor is not overwhelmed by constant price quotation, by Mr. Market's ceaseless urgings to buy or sell. Rather, the disciplined investor applies his or her own analysis in identifying mispriced stocks and adheres to a long-term time horizon, confident that the stock market will eventually revert to its professed role as a machine for crystallizing expected future cash flows and, ultimately, will reward those businesses with a sustainable earnings profile. The value investor must, as a colleague noted of Keynes' own temperament, maintain a "robust faith in the ultimate rightness of a policy based on reason and common sense." Or, as Warren Buffett comments in his homespun way, "[g]ames are won by players who focus on the playing field – not by those whose eyes are glued to the scoreboard."

DO-IT-YOURSELF

> *For my own part, I can certainly claim to be a Buddhist investor, in the sense of depending wholly on my own meditations.*
>
> —Keynes to a fellow stock investor, March 28, 1945

As Ben Graham observed, "Buying a neglected and therefore undervalued issue for profit generally proves a protracted and patience-trying experience," and the value investor must resist strong social forces that encourage conformism and a short-term mindset. Not only can constant price quotation distract undisciplined investors from the long-term merits of an investment, but stock market participants must also battle against an institutional apparatus geared to high turnover. Brokers and investment managers have a vested interest in promoting active markets, and even orthodox financial theory conspires with the speculator to assert the pre-eminence of short-term price movements over long-term income flow by defining "risk" as volatility in prices rather than volatility of earnings.

Value investors are not swayed by these factors. Rather, they recognize that the stock market is there to serve investors, not to instruct them. In the dark days of the early 1930s, after the stock market had suffered another of its sinking spells, Keynes remarked defiantly that:

> I do not draw from this the conclusion that a responsible investing body should every week cast panic glances over its list of securities to find one more victim to fling to the bears.

Value investors like Keynes rely on their own independent analysis rather than seeking guidance from the crowd. They practice, as Keynes did, "a certain continuity of policy" – a strategy that limits trading activity to those occasions when price departs widely from underlying value.

Stock market prices are relevant to the value investor as a benchmark against assessed intrinsic value, to determine whether a sufficient margin of safety exists. They are a potential entry or exit point for the investor, but past price patterns should not influence the investment decision. As Keynes said:

> it seems to me to be most important not to be upset out of one's permanent holdings by being too attentive to market movements ...

> Of course, it would be silly to ignore such things, but one's whole tendency is to be too much influenced by them.

It is a market truism that in times of crisis money moves from weak hands to strong hands – the disciplined investor must therefore cultivate, as Charlie Munger advises, a "disposition to own stocks without fretting."

GOING FOR IT

> *A nimble sixpence is better than a slow shilling.*
>
> —English proverb

One of the first trading ventures established by Keynes and "Foxy" Falk was the P.R. Finance Company, founded in early 1923 and engaged mainly in commodities speculation. The initials of the company – an allusion to the ancient Greek aphorism *Panta rei, ouden menei* ("All things flow, nothing abides") – were perhaps a subtle salute to the mercurial nature of the commodities market. In the stock market, too, all is in a state of flux – prices jump about and the intrinsic value of a stock alters as conditions affecting the underlying business change. Value investors, therefore, cannot let their professed bias toward a long-term investment horizon acquit them of the duty to remain vigilant, to be alert to changes in the value of stocks relative to their price.

A philosophy of "being quiet" – of trading only when a substantial gap is identified between a stock's intrinsic value and its quoted price – in no way implies a complacent investment style. In his role as chairman of National Mutual, Keynes repeatedly emphasized that investors cannot adopt a "set and forget" investment policy:

> The inactive investor who takes up an obstinate attitude about his holdings and refuses to change his opinion merely because facts

> and circumstances have changed is one who in the long run comes to grievous loss.

Value investors must, Keynes asserted, exercise "constant vigilance, constant revision of preconceived ideas, constant reaction to changes in the external situation." In stock market investing, he implied, the price of success is eternal vigilance.

The intelligent investor, by focusing only on those stocks within his or her circle of competence, will in fact be far more attuned to shifts in their relative value than market participants monitoring a much wider universe of securities. And by concentrating on a smaller pool of stocks, the value investor is in a better position to make a judgment on the merits of a particular security and act decisively. One observer of Keynes' methods with the King's College Chest Fund noted that:

> The great point about King's has been that when a good opportunity is pointed out to them, they "go for it." The swiftness of decision which marked their policy is due to Mr. Keynes.

Nicholas Davenport, a fellow board member at National Mutual, agreed that Keynes' stock market success was due to "beating the other fellow to the gun," adding that "I have never known a man so quick off the mark in the stock exchange race." Value investing, conducted properly, is not unlike Keynes' beloved cricket – vast longueurs occasionally punctuated by episodes of intense activity.

DEBT-DEFYING

> *Creditors are a superstitious sect, great observers of set days and times.*
>
> —Benjamin Franklin, *Poor Richard's Almanack*

During the effervescent days of the late 1920s – when Keynes still clung to the tenets of momentum investing, attempting to anticipate the anticipations of others, flitting in and out of the market – well over half of his investment portfolio was underwritten by borrowings. The idea was that he could leverage his bets on the financial exchanges – by borrowing money to speculate on the currency, commodity, and stock markets, Keynes would multiply his capital gains if his hunches were correct. Although he enjoyed intermittent success during these years, Keynes found that – like Irving Fisher, Ben Graham, and millions of others operating on credit during the Great Boom – leverage also works in reverse.

To take an extreme example, an investor buying a security on a 10 percent margin – that is, 90 percent of the purchase price is supported by borrowings – requires just a 10 percent increase in stock price to double his or her money. But with this greater potential reward comes a commensurate increase in risk – a 10 percent decline in price will effectively wipe out *all* the investor's capital contribution. Leverage works when markets are rising but can be catastrophic when they are falling. Margin loans and other forms of credit are an essential adjunct to many speculators' tool kits – they often work on fine margins, and borrowing funds allows them to raise the stakes on their stock market wagers. The power of leverage gives these game players the chance to potentially magnify capital profits, while "market liquidity" confers the illusion that there exists a fire escape should things get too hot.

The problem with fire escapes, however, is that they do not work particularly well when everyone is rushing the door at the same time. Those who believe that they can divine the tides of sentiment are often caught short when the market suddenly turns. Empirical evidence has, broadly speaking, failed to identify any single news factor that could explain some of the great "corrections" of the last century: the Crash of October 1929, "Black Monday" in 1987, the bursting of the dot-com bubble in March 2000. Those investors with leveraged positions – where market exposure far exceeded real capital resources – found themselves with financial obligations they simply could not meet. As Warren Buffett dryly comments, "You only find out who is swimming naked when the tide goes out."

Value investors – those who buy a stock on the expectation that, in the longer term, its quoted price will rise to meet intrinsic value – are particularly circumscribed when it comes to borrowings. Keynes observed that the market can stay irrational longer than game players can stay solvent – Alan Greenspan, the former Chair of the US Federal Reserve, made his famous "irrational exuberance" remark in 1996, more than three years before the dot-com bubble finally burst. The value investor must therefore be prepared to wait potentially considerable periods before the stock market weighing machine usurps the voting machine. Keynes consequently concluded that:

> an investor who proposes to ignore near-term market fluctuations needs greater resources for safety and must not operate on so large a scale, if at all, with borrowed money.

Something of a debt junkie in the 1920s and early 1930s, Keynes considerably reduced his borrowings in the latter part of his investment career, with loans constituting around 10 percent of assets in the last years of his life. This financial conservatism is repeated in the practices of Berkshire Hathaway, which, as Charlie Munger comments, is "chicken about buying stocks on margin." As Munger suggests, "The ideal is to borrow in a way no temporary thing can disturb you."

MIND CONTROL

> *I still suffer incurably from attributing an unreal rationality to other people's feelings and behavior*
>
> —Keynes, *My Early Beliefs*

Value investors require a dispassionate framework for investment decision-making, one that screens them from the insidious effects of animal spirits and short-termism. As Warren Buffett comments:

> Investing is not a game where the guy with the 160 IQ beats the guy with the 130 IQ ... Once you have ordinary intelligence, what you need is the temperament to control the urges that get other people into trouble in investing.

Cultivating the correct temperament – one that couples, in Buffett's words, "good business judgment with an ability to insulate thoughts and behavior from the super-contagious emotions that swirl about the marketplace" – requires the investor to focus on just two variables, the price and the intrinsic value of a stock.

The intelligent investor, although skeptical of the stock market's ability to always price securities correctly, nevertheless maintains an appropriately humble outlook. The investor not only accepts that on many – if not most – occasions the market is approximately efficient in terms of pricing, but also remains firmly within his or her circle of competence. Similarly, the investor does not succumb to the trait of overconfidence. Adam Smith, in his seminal work *The Wealth of Nations*, wryly remarked on:

> The overweening conceit which the greater part of men have of their own abilities ... and ... their absurd presumption in their own good Fortune ... There is no man living, who, when in tolerable health and spirits, has not some share of it. The chance of gain is by every man more or less overvalued, and the chance of loss is by most men undervalued.

Empirical evidence supports Smith's insight – individuals typically exaggerate their skills (to take an everyday example, considerably more than half of survey respondents believe they are much better drivers than the average motorist), and harbor overly optimistic views in respect of future events (research has shown, for instance, that game show contestants massively overestimate their chances of success).

GUILT-EDGED SECURITIES

> *In the stock market the facts of any situation come to us through a curtain of human emotions.*
>
> —Bernard Baruch, *My Own Story*

In addition to the traits of overconfidence and overoptimism, there are other cognitive biases that may affect investor behavior. Most important, perhaps, is the "endowment effect" – the tendency for people to apply an "ownership premium" to their possessions. A simple experiment conducted by the economist Richard Thaler – which showed that the average asking price of an object already owned by a person, in this case a coffee mug, was more than double the offer price of an equivalent object they did not yet own – illustrates the general principle that an individual will typically demand significantly more to give up something they already hold than they would be willing to pay to acquire the very same object.

In a similar manner, many stock market players appear to invest more than just dollars into their securities – a well-performed stock may garner positive emotional associations, and consequently the stockholder may be reluctant to sell his or her "pet" even when the quoted price far exceeds assessed intrinsic value. Conversely, an underperforming stock – whatever its future prospects – may be sold by the rash investor, rather in the manner of a guilty party anxious to dispose of incriminating evidence. Perhaps a more likely scenario – in light of findings by behavioral economists that financial losses exacted more than twice the emotional impact of an equivalent gain – is that some stockholders may be reluctant to sell under- performing securities, even those unlikely to return to favor, because to do so would crystallize a loss and confirm their original investment error.

The intelligent investor does not lapse into these episodes of transference, and remembers that, as Warren Buffett puts it rather poignantly, "The stock doesn't know you own it." Value investors focus on the perceived value of a stock based on expected future cash flows, and do not fixate on the original acquisition price. If investors are to anchor themselves to any particular number, it should be to anticipated future earnings rather than historical prices. The decision to buy, sell, or hold a security should be determined by reference to "a policy based on reason," one free from the taint of animal spirits and emotional baggage. Value investors concentrate unwaveringly on the economics of the underlying business – they are security analysts rather than insecurity analysts.

PRIDE GOETH BEFORE DESTRUCTION . . .

> *While enthusiasm may be necessary for great accomplishments elsewhere, on Wall Street it almost invariably leads to disaster.*
>
> —Ben Graham, *The Intelligent Investor*

Aware of these psychological quirks, value investors work diligently within their circle of competence, practicing what Buffett terms "emotional discipline" and dealing only in stocks displaying a wide margin of safety. In an early press interview, Buffett compared investing to being in "a great big casino [where] everyone else is boozing." He suggested that if the intelligent investor can stick to Pepsi (or, given his subsequent acquisitions, Coke), then that individual will do fine. Charlie Munger made the same point in a letter to Wesco shareholders:

> It is remarkable how much long-term advantage people like us have gotten by trying to be consistently not stupid, instead of

> trying to be very intelligent. There must be some wisdom in the folk saying, "It's the strong swimmers who drown."

It was once remarked of Foxy Falk and his hyperintelligent merchant banking colleagues that "their brains make them dangerous, for they arrive at their errors more rapidly." Mere intelligence is not sufficient for stock market success – the disciplined investor must possess a robust and objective framework for investment decision-making, and a temperament that, as Keynes suggested, exhibits "much patience and courage." In a similar vein, Ben Graham noted that "the investor's chief problem – and even his worst enemy – is likely to be himself," and suggested that the successful stock market participant requires not only intelligence and an understanding of value investing principles, but also – and most importantly – "firmness of character."

FOREWARNED, FOREARMED

> *The modern organization of the capital market requires for the holder of quoted equities much more nerve, patience, and fortitude than from the holder of wealth in other forms.*
>
> —Keynes to the King's College Estates Committee, May 8, 1938

The man who confirmed the primacy of money in economic theory thought very little of it in practice. To Keynes it was nothing more than a means to an end, a passport to the possibilities of life. It was this equivocal, utilitarian attitude to moneymaking that bestowed the sangfroid required for a businesslike attitude to stock market investing. Keynes realized that successful stock market players could not be distracted by constant price quotations, which were driven, by definition, by the greediest buyers and most jittery sellers. Rather, investors needed to cultivate "a sense of proportion" – the confidence that, despite short-term gyrations, in the longer term the market would recognize and reward those stocks with sustainable earnings.

Keynes cautioned that the intelligent investor must think independently, unaffected by the views of the pack. The disciplined stock-picker cannot be seduced by the siren calls of continuous price quotation, and must negotiate a course between excessive activity and an unresponsive passivity. The market is no respecter of the debt-servicing timetables of creditors, the expiry dates of derivatives, or the margin requirements of brokers – the intelligent investor does not, therefore, give hostages to fortune by borrowing excessively or relying on options.

Investing, in the style of Keynes and Buffett, may seem an easy game, but this simplicity of approach is deceptive. The investor must remain uninfluenced by the bipolar tendencies of the market and ensure that he or she is not tainted by the pathogen of animal spirits. As Keynes remarked to a colleague, successful investing may in fact require "more temperament than logic" – the ability to invest with one's head rather than one's glands, to paraphrase a Buffett observation. The intelligent investor – armed with the knowledge of concepts such as intrinsic value and safety first, and aware of the stock market's dual personality as a voting machine and a weighing machine – will be much better placed to cultivate the right temperament for successful investing.

14.

POST MORTEM

THE ESTABLISHMENT REBEL

I agree with everything in this if not *is put in front of every statement.*

—Keynes' verdict on a government memorandum

THERE IS A STORY that toward the end of Maynard Keynes' life, when he had once again returned to the warm and secure embrace of the Establishment, he was gently reproved for becoming orthodox in his old age. Keynes gave short shrift to such a foolish charge – "Orthodoxy has at last caught up with me," he replied with customary aplomb. After innumerable battles with what he mockingly called "sound finance", Keynes was justified in claiming, finally, to be on the right side of conventional wisdom. The central conclusions of *The General Theory* – that financial markets can misbehave, that disturbances in the world of money can blight the real economy, and that government intervention is required to remedy these dislocations – were accepted with the same certitude that classical dogma had been accorded only a few years earlier, and the "Keynesian consensus" ruled the developed world for the next three decades.

It has taken far longer for Keynes' views on stock market investing to move into the mainstream. Orthodox financial theorists had doggedly maintained that modern financial exchanges are efficient mechanisms for pricing securities and that one share is as good a bet as another. The emergence of "behavioral finance" – integrating psychological insights with economics – has at last overturned the flawless fairy tale world of classical economics, in which all men are not only unfailingly rational, but also invested with a divine omnipotence. Once again, *The General Theory* has proved the harbinger for an intellectual revolution.

As Keynes would no doubt have asserted, however, a set of principles are only as good as their practical efficacy. Keynes himself was prepared to change his mind when the facts warranted such a move – like his sometimes sparring partner, sometimes ally, Winston Churchill, Keynes never developed indigestion from eating his words. Ever the pragmatist, each year he applied the blowtorch of analysis to his investment performance, "partly with a view to comparing our [stock market] experiences with those of other investors and partly to discover what lessons were to be learnt." These "post mortems", as he termed them, were valuable not only in determining "whence the satisfactory results came," but also – and perhaps more importantly – in identifying where performance was susceptible to improvement.

Although Keynes was one of the world's first institutional equity investors, and was widely acclaimed during his lifetime for his mastery of financial markets in practice as well as in theory, the man's investment performance had not been subject to detailed empirical analysis until recently. Research from three British academics – David Chambers, Elroy Dimson and Justin Foo – confirms that Keynes was an outstandingly successful long-term stock market investor, outperforming the broader market by a wide margin over a multi-decade period. In particular, the authors of the study identify a radical change in fortune for Keynes' stock portfolios – from significant underperformance during the 1920s when he practiced a top-down "credit cycling" approach, to substantial outperformance in later years after adopting a bottom-up value investing style.

HAVING A FLUTTER

> *As regards the Railway Stocks, I am amused that they are at last dear enough for Francis to be inclined to buy them.*
>
> —Keynes to his stockbroker, January 1943

Keynes' omnivorous interests in the wider world were matched by those in the financial arena. Not only was he involved in investment and speculation in various capacities – on his own account, as College bursar with a large degree of discretion, and as a board member with less influence on investment decisions – but his moneymaking activities encompassed many different types of assets, from pig lard to preferred stock. Most importantly for our purposes, Keynes' investment style also changed radically in the early 1930s – from one of market timing to a more measured policy of value investing.

This eclectic approach, although providing a broad base from which to develop his theories on investment, also highlights the importance of selecting an appropriate benchmark to assess Keynes' stock market performance. Some of Keynes' financial ventures, such as the P.R. Finance Company, can be ignored on the basis that they were principally involved in currency or commodities speculation. Others can be dismissed due to Keynes' limited tenure as an investment adviser or board member – for example, Keynes left the A.D. Investment Trust, the first investment company he founded with Foxy Falk, in late 1927, well before his transfiguration into value investor. Likewise, Keynes effectively absented himself from an active management role at the Independent Investment Company in the mid-1930s and resigned from his position as Chairman of the National Mutual in 1938.

In some undertakings Keynes was hindered by institutional inertia and a stubbornly reactionary mindset. A letter from the Provost of Eton College to Keynes captures the frustrations of group decision-making:

> I find Governing Bodies meetings usually very entertaining. I like to hear the naked covetousness with which you recommend Southern Preferred Stock, the austere puritanism with which Lubbock meets such suggestions and the tergiversation of Ridley, who, agreeing with Lubbock, nevertheless votes with you because it is a poor heart that never rejoices and one must have a flutter sometimes.

Keynes' advocacy of "buying against the stream" more often than not met with fierce resistance from his fellow board members – as Keynes commented wearily, "All orthodox suggestions are too expensive, and all unorthodox are too unorthodox, so I am rather discouraged about making any further suggestion."

THE CHEST FUND

> *Most people are too timid and too greedy, too impatient and too nervous about their investments, the fluctuations in the paper value of which can so easily obliterate the results of so much honest effort, to take long views or to place even as much reliance as they reasonably might on the dubieties of the long period; the apparent certainties of the short period, however deceptive we may suspect them to be, are much more attractive."*
>
> ——Keynes, *A Treatise on Money*

There were only two investment concerns that focused on stocks and in which Keynes retained a large measure of decision-making discretion. The first was the Provincial Insurance Company, a small company "rather in the nature of a family affair," according to Keynes. Donald Moggridge, editor of Keynes' *Collected Writings,* notes that:

> [Keynes] was an extremely active director [of Provincial] throughout the years after 1930 ... On investments, Keynes had fairly complete discretion within the guidelines set by the board at its monthly meetings and successfully persuaded the firm of the virtues of equities.

As Keynes observed with evident satisfaction in a memorandum for the Provincial board in 1938, the company "gave a good thrashing" to comparable market indices while under his stewardship. Keynes' influence on the board declined, however, after 1940, when he was called back to the Treasury.

The best benchmark for assessing Keynes' stock market performance is undoubtedly the King's College Discretionary Portfolio, largely represented by the Chest Fund – for not only did it focus on equities, but management of the fund remained with Keynes until his death. Moreover, this portfolio would seem to faithfully represent Keynes' investment principles and preferences, as its composition largely mirrored his personal holdings, with around 80 percent by value of Keynes' private portfolio also held by the King's endowment. The Chest Fund, established in June 1920 and capitalized at £30,000, was one of the few college funds permitted to invest in stocks, and Keynes exploited this freedom to deliver astonishing results over a multidecade period.

Taking 1931 as the base year – admittedly a relatively low point in the Fund's fortunes, but also on the assumption that Keynes' value investment style began around this time – the Chest Fund recorded a roughly tenfold increase in value in the fifteen years to 1945, compared with a virtual nil return for the Standard & Poor's 500 Average and a mere doubling of the London industrial index over the same period. This vast outperformance relative to comparable indices is even more impressive in light of the fact that all income generated by the Chest Fund was spent on college building works and the repayment of loans – in other words, the capital appreciation from £30,000 in 1920 to around £380,000 at the time of Keynes' death solely comprised capital gains on the portfolio.

A SURVEY

Results must be judged by what one does on the round journey.

—Keynes to a National Mutual board member, March 18, 1938

The quantitative study undertaken by Chambers, Dimson and Foo focused on Keynes' management of the Discretionary Portfolio, which included the Chest Fund, over the quarter century from 1921 to 1946. Basing their analysis on annual Investment Reports of the King's College endowment, the academics confirm Keynes' reputation as a masterful stock market investor – over his 25 year tenure as investment manager, Keynes generated an annual return of 16 percent, compared to a 10.4 percent annual return for the benchmarked index. Beating the market by a significant margin over a period that included the Crash of 1929, the Great Depression and the Second World War was an impressive feat in itself, but these headline figures mask an even more remarkable performance in the 1930s and 1940s, when Keynes switched to a bottom-up investment style in his search for radically mispriced stocks.

The study bluntly notes that over the 1920s Keynes' momentum trading approach "generated disappointing returns ... [with] no evidence of any market-timing ability". During this decade, the Discretionary Portfolio underperformed the broader market by an average of 5.3 percent annually, whereas Keynes' rebirth as a value-driven investor coincided with substantial outperformance against the benchmark index from 1933 to 1946. The difference in performance is similarly stark when considered on a year-by-year basis – across the quarter of a century that he managed the Discretionary Portfolio, Keynes underperformed the market in only six years, with four of those years crowded into the 1920s.

The research also charts Keynes' steady progression towards a buy-and-hold investment style. Practicing his policy of "faithfulness," Keynes' annual stock turnover fell over time – averaging 55 percent in the 1920s (that is, turning over his stock portfolio in just under two years), slowing to 30 percent throughout the 1930s (turnover decreasing to less than once every three years), and falling to only 14 percent in the 1940s. In addition to being a long-term holder of equities, Keynes' allocations to individual stocks within the Discretionary Portfolio were highly concentrated, with the largest five shareholdings comprising 46 percent of total portfolio value in the 1920s and 49 percent in the 1930s, then falling back slightly to 33 percent in the 1940s.

Although Keynes favored putting most of his eggs in a relatively small number of baskets, he attained some measure of diversification through his increasingly large purchases of United States-listed shares. Keynes' first investment in American common stocks was in early 1929, and the allocation to U.S. stocks steadily increased throughout the 1930s – averaging 33 percent throughout the decade, and comprising fully half of the portfolio by 1939. Keynes' growing appetite for offshore holdings was finally curbed in the early 1940s, when the British Treasury obliged domestic investors to sell American stocks in order to boost U.S. dollar reserves.

KODAK MOMENT

> *When anyone asks me how I can best describe my experience in nearly forty years at sea, I merely say, uneventful. Of course there have been winter gales, and storms and fog and the like. But in all my experience, I have never been in any accident ... or any sort worth speaking about. I have seen but one vessel in distress in all my years at sea. I never saw a wreck and never have been wrecked nor was I ever in any predicament that threatened to end in disaster of any sort.*
>
> —Edward Smith, Captain of RMS *Titanic*, 1907

In adopting value investing over momentum trading, Keynes completely changed the direction of his vision – rather than slipstreaming behind past trends, from the 1930s onward he looked forward, focusing on a specific company's "ultimate earning power" when assessing opportunities. Realizing that stock valuation was as much an art as a science – and dismissive of analysts who claimed to conjure a price target down to the last cent – Keynes searched for "ultra-favourites" with robust long-term earnings potential, where price had seemingly diverged from future prospects. In a similar manner, Warren Buffett favors companies with a sustainable competitive advantage – in his words, "great companies with dominant positions, whose franchise is hard to duplicate and [with] tremendous staying power."

Keynes and Buffett's more qualitative approach to stock selection contrasts with that of Ben Graham, who relied on a rigorous quantitative framework centered around book value. However, in a world where a company's competitive edge is increasingly attributable to intangible assets such as intellectual property and human capital, a more flexible approach is required. Keynes himself was overweight in the technology stocks of his day – such as automobile and aircraft manufacturing, pharmaceuticals and power generation – and often employed novel valuation metrics when scrutinising opportunities. As Chambers, Dimson and Foo note:

> he valued Austin Motor shares employing not only a conventional measure such as earnings yield but also market capitalisation per unit produced. According to his calculations in October 1933, Austin traded at a 67% discount to General Motors.

In today's environment where increasing returns to scale accrue to many internet and technology companies due to network effects, the appropriate focus is increasingly forward rather than backward – on sustainable future earnings rather than historic balance sheet measures.

As Warren Buffett noted in a magazine article:

> The key to investing is not assessing how much an industry is going to affect society, or how much it will grow, but rather determining the competitive advantage of any given company and, above all, the durability of that advantage.

Many apparently robust commercial "moats" in fact turn out to be Maginot Lines during capitalism's perennial gales of creative destruction, as competitive attrition eliminates the less fit. Kodak, for example, was a leading member of the blue-chip "Nifty Fifty" stock cohort in the 1960s and 1970s, and at the time was rated as one of the world's five most valuable brands. However the company, developer of the first digital camera, was blindsided by the introduction of smartphone cameras earlier this century and ultimately filed for bankruptcy protection in 2011. The Kodak experience is a reminder that, due to competitive dynamics, some high growth sectors – whether it be internal combustion automobiles in Keynes' time, or electric vehicles in our era – will not necessarily offer compelling individual investment opportunities.

DODGING STUMERS

Rule No. 1: Never lose money. Rule No. 2: Never forget Rule 1.

—Warren Buffett

Two broad trends are discernible in Keynes' stock market performance – the first is that, as his biographer Robert Skidelsky notes, "the more directly under Keynes' control the investments were, the better they performed," the second is the marked improvement in investment performance dating from the early 1930s. As Donald Moggridge observes in his assessment of the performance of Keynes' personal holdings:

> Whereas in the 1920s Keynes was generally less successful than the market, after 1929 his investments (treating Wall Street and London separately) outperformed the market on 21 of the 30 available accounting years and did so cumulatively by a large margin.

Keynes attributed his stock market success to "a safety first policy" which resulted in "the avoidance of 'stumers' with which many investment lists are disfigured." In a letter to a colleague at Provincial, Keynes expanded on the importance of minimizing losses:

> there had scarcely been a single case of any large-scale loss. There had been big fluctuations in market prices. But none of the main investments had, in the end, turned out otherwise than all right. Thus, against the profits which inevitably accumulate, there were comparatively few losses to offset. Virtually *all* our big holdings had come right.

Keynes' investment performance confirms that successful stock market investing is, as Charles Ellis described it in the title of one of his books, a "loser's game." The key task for the investor is to *avoid mistakes* – this is done by working within one's circle of competence and ensuring that a substantial margin of safety exists in respect of each stock purchase. As Ben Graham commented in *The Intelligent Investor*, "The really dreadful losses ... were realized in those common-stock issues where the buyer forgot to ask 'How much?'"

Putting aside his earlier dismissal of "City men" as overpaid and sometimes bumbling intermediaries, Keynes became a fervent consumer of broker notes in his quest to better identify future "pets." This desktop research was supplemented by more strenuous inquiries – leveraging his Establishment contacts, Keynes insisted on meetings with the management of companies in which he was interested, and sometimes engaged with government policymakers to better understand the competitive landscape. Such was Keynes' commitment to active, bottom-up research that in the early 1930s he undertook two study trips to the United States, when a transatlantic cruise averaged five days, in order to understand the American market first-hand.

THROUGH THICK AND THIN

> *I made my money by selling too soon.*
>
> —Bernard Baruch (attributed)

If some commentators have found fault with Keynes' investment performance, it was in his apparent inability to dispose of overpriced stocks. One academic described Keynes as a "one-armed contrarian who bought at the bottom but could never get out at the top" – an investor who could identify underpriced stocks but was less adroit when it came to jettisoning overpriced paper. Keynes was perhaps aware of his particular susceptibility to holding on to individual stocks even after they had become too expensive based on his own value investing principles. In a post mortem written for King's College, he defended himself as follows:

> One may be, and no doubt is, inclined to be too slow to sell one's pets after they have had most of their rise. But looking back I don't blame myself *much* on this score; – it would have been easy to lose a great deal more by selling them too soon.

In early 1936, for example, Keynes noted at the annual meeting of National Mutual unit holders that prices of British industrial shares were very high and presumed:

> not merely a maintenance of the present industrial activity for an indefinite period to come but a substantial further improvement. Not that many people actually believe this, but each is hopeful of unloading on the other fellow in good time.

Despite this unequivocal view, Keynes held on to most of his stocks and suffered a significant fall in portfolio value when the stock markets experienced yet another severe decline in 1937. With reassuring infrequency, Warren Buffett also candidly pleads guilty to the same crime. "I made a big mistake in not selling several of our larger holdings during The Great Bubble," he confessed in the wake of the internet boom and bust of the late 1990s. Keynes' and Buffett's errors of omission in this regard are a reminder to investors that, as Charlie Munger stresses, "If you stick with stocks that are underpriced, you must keep moving or switching them around as they move closer to their true value."

Keynes' tendency to hold on to some of his pets for too long may have been due to his overwhelmingly optimistic nature – as Clive Bell commented, "Maynard's judgment would have been as sound as his intellect was powerful had it really been detached; but Maynard was an incorrigible optimist." All investors are, of course, optimists to some extent – they defer present consumption, commending capital to the uncharted land of the future, in the hope of a return. As it turns out, Keynes' inclination toward a "a steadfast holding ... through thick and thin" was also his greatest strength as an investor – somewhat ironically for a man who remarked that in the long-run we are all dead, Keynes was particularly scornful of the stock market's insistence on taking the short view. Time in the market, rather than market-timing, would prove to be a key element in his success in the investing arena.

15.

A SUMMING UP

STOCK MARKET JUJITSU

The way is to avoid what is strong and to strike at what is weak.

—Sun Tzu, *The Art of War*

KEYNES' EXPERIENCES ON THE stock market read like some sort of morality play – an ambitious young man, laboring under the ancient sin of hubris, loses almost everything in his furious pursuit of wealth; suitably humbled, our protagonist, now wiser for the experience, applies his considerable intellect to the situation and discovers what he believes to be the one true path to stock market success. In his later incarnation, Keynes looked beyond short-term price trends and events, instead focusing on the long-term earnings potential of a stock and adopting a steadfast holding of his "pets."

The practice of value investing involves identifying those stocks displaying a wide gap between quoted prices and a reasonable estimate of future income potential, and often requires the investor to battle against the prevailing currents of crowd sentiment. The value investor favors a long-term investment horizon, and is content to wait for the froth of constantly quoted prices to eventually reconcile with the reality of earnings. Keynes' additional gloss to the value investing canon is a policy of portfolio concentration – of putting one's eggs in only a handful of baskets – a strategy practiced by Buffett, but not by some other notable value investors, such as Ben Graham.

In a memorandum written for the King's College Estates Committee in 1938, Keynes set out the most concise summary of his stock market investment philosophy:

> I believe now that successful investment depends on three principles:
>
> 1. a careful selection of a few investments (or a few types of investment) having regard to their cheapness in relation to their probable actual and potential *intrinsic* value over a period of years ahead and in relation to alternative investments at the time;
> 2. a steadfast holding of these in fairly large units through thick and thin, perhaps for several years, until either they have fulfilled their promise or it is evident that they were purchased on a mistake;
> 3. a *balanced* investment position, i.e. a variety of risks in spite of individual holdings being large, and if possible opposed risks (e.g. a holding of gold shares amongst other equities, since they are likely to move in opposite directions when there are general fluctuations).

In effect, Keynes proposed a form of stock market jujitsu. Rather than trying to run just ahead of the inconstant mob, attempting to pick the bull and bear tacks of the stock market before they actually happen, Keynes determined that a better approach for disciplined investors was to use the kinetic energy of an irrational market to their own advantage. Instead of contributing to market volatility, caught up in the pendulum swings of sentiment, the value investor stands apart from the wildly flailing market and waits for it to overbalance. When excessive exuberance or pessimism throws up a "stunner" or a "grand-slam home run," the intelligent investor – working within his circle of competence and confident of a wide margin of safety – can act decisively and commit a relatively large amount of capital to the transaction.

THE PRINCIPLES

> *Everything interested him because everything in his mind fitted instantaneously into its place in the conflict between Wisdom and Folly.*
>
> —Treasury colleague on Keynes

Keynes' stock market activities were but one aspect of an enormously productive life. As the *New York Times* noted in its obituary on Keynes, in addition to his better known accomplishments as an economist and statesman, he also cultivated an astoundingly wide range of interests in other fields:

> He was a Parliamentary orator of high order, a historian and devotee of music, the drama and the ballet. While at Cambridge University, he founded an arts theatre there because he wanted to go to a good theatre. A successful farmer, he was an expert on development of grass feeding stuffs.

Drawing on his vast and divergent knowledge base, and emboldened by a refusal to walk the worn paths of convention, Keynes distilled a set of investment principles that not only brought him great personal prosperity but also provided a template for stock market investors generally.

Keynes' six key investment rules, which have been embraced by some of the world's most successful stock market investors, suggest that the informed value investor should:

1. Focus on the estimated *intrinsic value* of a stock – as represented by the projected earnings of the particular security – rather than attempt to divine market trends.
2. Ensure that a sufficiently large *margin of safety* – the difference between a stock's assessed intrinsic value and price – exists in respect of purchased stocks.
3. Apply independent judgment in valuing stocks, which may often imply a *contrarian* investment policy.
4. Limit transaction costs and ignore the distractions of constant price quotation by maintaining *a steadfast holding* of stocks.
5. Practice a policy of *portfolio concentration* by committing relatively large sums of capital to stock market "stunners."
6. Maintain the appropriate *temperament* by balancing "equanimity and patience" with the ability to act decisively.

Keynes' investment principles are disarmingly simple, and may seem at first instance to be little more than applied common sense, especially when compared to the elaborate mathematics and complex concepts of modern financial theory. Value investing does not rely on academic esoterica like "beta," the "capital asset pricing model," or "optimized portfolios" – rather, it focuses on just two variables: price and intrinsic value. As Warren Buffett has remarked, "It's a little like spending eight years in divinity school and having somebody tell you that the ten commandments were all that counted."

Keynes was aware of the insidious power of accepted wisdom, its ability to "ramify ... into every corner of our minds." Despite recent incursions by new disciplines such as behavioral finance, orthodox theory obstinately asserts that financial markets are broadly efficient – as Buffett notes with palpable resignation, "Ships will sail around the world but the Flat Earth society will flourish." Yet the sustained success of value investors such as Maynard Keynes and, more recently, Warren Buffett is perhaps the most eloquent testimony to the inadequacy of orthodox dogma.

EVERY CROWD HAS A SILVER LINING

> *If God didn't want them sheared, he would not have made them sheep.*
> —The bandit-leader Calvera, *The Magnificent Seven*

Ben Graham applied a measure of anthropomorphic sleight of hand to beget that embodiment of an irrational stock exchange, Mr. Market. Warren Buffett, Graham's most renowned disciple, provides a concise character sketch of this creation:

> [Mr. Market] has incurable emotional problems. At times he feels euphoric and can see only the favorable factors affecting the business. When in that mood, he names a very high buy–sell price because he fears that you will snap up his interest and rob him of imminent gains. At other times he is depressed and can see nothing but trouble ahead for both the business and the world. On these occasions he will name a very low price, since he is terrified that you will unload your interest on him.

Mr. Market is riddled with a complex array of character pathologies. Afflicted by periodic "waves of irrational psychology," he can suffer from alternate bouts of mania and depression. Mr. Market can metamorphose into Mr. Magoo – an extremely myopic character, congenitally unable to take the long view. And he can also be psychosomatic, with disturbances in his state of mind impacting not only the stock market but also the real economy.

In contract law, agreements with individuals of an unsound mind are generally unenforceable. In the dog-eat-dog world of the stock market, however, investors are free to exploit the periodic madness of others. Rather than being influenced by short-term price fluctuations – by Mr. Market's interminable yammerings – intelligent investors instead concentrate on the perceived underlying value of a business. The phrase "value investing," then, is something of a tautology, for all true investing – as opposed to speculation – involves an assessment of underlying value. The value investor – realizing that a stock price is transitory, a snapshot of jostling views and emotions – views Mr. Market's prices as nothing more than a possible entry or exit point on to the market.

Price trends and market fashions are of no concern to the disciplined stock-picker – instead, the investor applies his or her own independent analysis to the investment decision-making process. Intelligent investors buy for value reasons and capitalize on the mistakes of those who do not. Stocks, for these individuals, are not mere tracings on a chart or icons on a smartphone screen, but real entities producing real goods and services. At Berkshire Hathaway's annual meetings, Buffett emphasizes the ultimate concreteness of his stock holdings by gulping Coke, offering discounts to Berkshire-owned jewelry stores, and promoting the company's candy shops. Value investors focus on the attributes of the *business* – particularly future earnings – and when Mr. Market casts aside his accountant's eye-shade and dons his party hat, or assumes dark robes of mourning, they search carefully for the radically mispriced bet.

CASINO CAPITALISM

> *I and other economic forecasters didn't understand that markets are prone to wild and even deranging mood swings that are uncoupled from any underlying rational basis.*
>
> —Alan Greenspan, 2013

Keynes, the Poet of Uncertainty, recognised that in the arena of investing there are many events for which "there is no scientific basis on which to form any calculable probability whatever." Investors simply cannot be the idealized *homo economicus* of classical theory, making a cold calculation of expected outcomes multiplied by expected probabilities. Because of this unavoidable uncertainty, most stock market participants are overly focused on near term factors and prey to the winds of sentiment. This tendency is even more marked in game players with, as Keynes put it, "no special knowledge of the circumstances, either actual or prospective, of the business" in which they own a part share. Keynes believed that this lack of knowledge increased the market's fickleness and its propensity to overreact to new information, "since there will be no strong roots of conviction to hold [a valuation] steady."

If anything, Mr. Market's manias and meltdowns are even more pronounced in our "democratized" investing world – enabled by smartphone apps replete with technicolor screens and exploding in a cloudburst of confetti upon swiping "buy" – that can have the effect of fostering groupthink and narrowing the focus to the very short term. Studies have shown that American stock exchanges display clear evidence of "excess volatility," where securities prices are considerably more variable than the underlying fundamentals. Moreover, excess volatility in stock prices has increased significantly in recent decades – as Andrew Haldane, Chief Economist at the Bank of England, notes, "[u]p until the 1960s prices were around twice as volatile as fundamentals ...

[but since] 1990 they have been anywhere between six and ten times more volatile." The digital herd, spurred on by gamified stock trading apps and operating within the echo chamber of the internet, exacerbates the risk of informational cascades and distorted securities prices.

While financial markets and products have changed significantly since Keynes' time, underlying human psychology has not. We have brains evolved for life on the savanna, not the abstract plane of symbols and numbers, and this brave new world of hyperkinetic markets and disembodied symbols increases the scope for irrational behavior and market volatility. Neuroscience demonstrates that we are not the clinical calculators idealized in conventional financial theory, but rather flesh-and-blood creatures, with hormones such as cortisol and testosterone coursing through our bodies in varying measures, affecting both our decision-making and risk appetite. An undeclared civil war rages in our head, a conflict between our instinctive limbic system and our more reflective neocortex. As Nobel Prize–winning psychologist and economist Daniel Kahneman notes, humans have an "almost unlimited ability to ignore our ignorance," taking cognitive short-cuts that result in predictably irrational behavior.

GET RICH SLOWLY

> *To do nothing at all is the most difficult thing in the world.*
>
> —Oscar Wilde

For these reasons, value investors determine that it is inadvisable to invest side-by-side with Mr. Market, instead electing to sit across the table from him and wait for an offer that simply cannot be refused. This posture requires tremendous patience and fortitude – as Warren Buffett notes:

> Though markets are generally rational, they occasionally do crazy things. Seizing the opportunities then offered does not require

> great intelligence, a degree in economics or a familiarity with Wall Street jargon such as alpha and beta. What investors then need instead is an ability to both disregard mob fears or enthusiasms and to focus on a few simple fundamentals. A willingness to look unimaginative for a sustained period – or even to look foolish – is also essential.

Appropriately for a custodian of King's College – the ultimate long-term investor, founded before Christopher Columbus made landfall in the Americas – Keynes, after a couple of false starts, also took the long view in the investment game.

He realised that stock markets are what we would now call an "emergent phenomena," where "the whole is not equal to the sum of parts, ... small changes produce large effects, the assumptions of a uniform and homogenous continuum are not satisfied." In practice, this means that stock markets do not exhibit the smooth symmetry of a classic Bell curve with "thin tails" of extreme moves from the mean – rather, stock prices generate "fat tails" representing a much higher probability of outlier events. Studies have demonstrated that relatively few trading days contribute to the bulk of total stock market returns – Keynes himself was schooled the hard way that the stock market could avalanche or spike in an instant, and that a value investor's edge in a world of quicksilver, near frictionless markets was patience. He realised that market efficiency is ultimately a question of timing – that the weighing machine would triumph over the voting machine over the long term, or as investor and strategist Jeremy Grantham notes, "we wait for extreme situations and predict that they will become normal once again".

A long-term buy-and-hold investment approach, in addition to giving time for the market to re-assert its role as weighing machine rather than voting machine, also harnesses the tremendous cumulative power of compounding. Research by Professors Chambers, Dimson and Spaenjers on Keynes' art collection demonstrates the value creation potential of holding a suite of assets over the very long term – acquired for just under £13,000 during his lifetime, the collection has an estimated value of £76 million ($95 million) now. Keynes' contrarian escapade at the Paris showroom in 1918 seems to have been replicated in his other fine art acquisitions – the authors of a study on the performance of his art portfolio note that "[t]he collection performed especially well shortly after purchase, suggesting that Keynes was able to buy art at attractive prices." Perhaps more startling is the disproportionate role of positive outliers in contributing to overall portfolio performance – one item acquired for only £1.50 was valued at £20 million, or around $25 million, in 2019.

HERD ON THE STREET

> *Our stay-put behavior reflects our view that the stock market serves as a relocation center at which money is moved from the active to the patient.*
>
> —Warren Buffet, 1991 Berkshire Hathaway shareholder letter

As in the art world, so too in the stock market arena – a small number of securities generate the bulk of overall returns. Research indicates that the entire gain in developed stock markets is usually attributable to a mere handful of securities – finance academic Hendrik Bessembinder, for example, found that only 4 percent of U.S. stocks accounted for all of the net market returns over the 90 year period from 1926 to 2015. The best way to find these needles in stock market haystacks will be dependent on a particular investor's knowledge of the market and risk appetite. For those that possess the requisite expertise, temperament and time horizon, a concentrated portfolio of "loading up" on high-conviction pets – in the manner of Keynes and Warren Buffett – is a sound strategy.

However, Keynes also conceded that a policy of wide diversification – of "scattering one's investments over as many fields as possible" – would in fact be the best course of action for an individual with no special knowledge of the stock market. Warren Buffett similarly encourages unsophisticated investors to put their money, at regular intervals, into index funds that mimic broader market performance. In a letter to Berkshire Hathaway shareholders, Buffett explained that:

> The goal of the non-professional should not be to pick winners … but should rather be to own a cross-section of businesses that in aggregate are bound to do well … The main danger is that the timid or beginning investor will enter the market at a time of extreme exuberance and then become disillusioned when paper losses occur … The antidote to that kind of mistiming is for an investor to accumulate shares over a long period and never to sell when the news is bad and stocks are well off their highs.

Keynes and Buffett – both unconquerable optimists – formed the view that growth in the broader economy would ultimately be reflected in buoyant stock prices, and that everyman investors could benefit from this dynamic by casting the investing net widely.

An alternative route for the average investor seeking a more targeted exposure is to delegate decision-making to someone else. Berkshire Hathaway shareholders have been doing this for more than half a century – backing the investment wisdom of Warren Buffett and Charlie Munger – while other investors may opt for an active, bottom-up manager to steward their investments. Keynes was an immensely successful manager of the King's endowment largely because the College's investment committee was willing to look beyond near term price fluctuations and granted Keynes the autonomy to execute his highly focused, contrarian investment strategy. Unfortunately for investors today, behavioral finance experts have confirmed Keynes' lament that "it is better for reputation to fail conventionally than to succeed unconventionally."

Daniel Kahneman has noted that decision-makers acting as agents for others, such as financial advisers, "expect to have their decisions scrutinized with hindsight ... [and are therefore] driven to bureaucratic solutions – and to an extreme reluctance to take risks." Large fund managers can be driven by a form of "rational irrationality" – a desire to stick close the herd so as to reduce the risk of underperforming relative to peers. Only those innate contrarians, comfortable zigging when others zag, and supported by the right organizational structure, have the potential to break away from the investment pack.

In managing the King's endowment, Keynes was one of the first institutional managers to overwhelmingly favor the then nascent asset class of equities – Professors Chambers and Dimson found that the Discretionary Portfolio averaged a 75 percent share weighting in the 1920s, 57 percent in the 1930s, and 73 percent in the 1940s, far in excess of other endowments. Many other Cambridge and Oxford colleges did not diversify into stocks until after the Second World War, and even the more innovative American university portfolios generally recorded a stock allocation of less than 20 percent by the 1940s. Keynes argued that stocks represented "the live large-scale business and investment world of today," and this statement was largely true in his day. However, in recent times the stock market has become much less representative of the broader economy – the number of publicly traded companies in the U.S. has halved over the last 20 years, alternative funding sources such as private equity and venture capital have further eroded the listed stock universe, and in value terms stock markets are increasingly dominated by technology stocks. Given this contraction in the scope of listed markets, Keynes – an investment pioneer in every sense – would no doubt encourage investors diversify into alternative asset classes, for example exposure to highly defensive real assets such as forestry and farmland.

THE WHEEL TURNS

In Washington Lord Halifax
Whispered to Lord Keynes
"It's true they've all the money bags.
But we've got all the brains."
—Note passed around among the British loan negotiation team

In the summer of 1940, the treadmill of time seemed to have spun full revolution for Keynes. War had been declared the previous year, and once again Keynes found himself back in the Treasury. "Well here am I, like a recurring decimal, doing very similar work in the same place for a similar emergency," he lamented to an American banker in July 1942. As in the Great War, Britain again found herself a supplicant at the feet of Uncle Sam, and this time Keynes – given "a sort of roving commission" by the Chancellor – was assigned the task of negotiating the American loans. The quintessential Englishman, a man of vast independent wealth, was dispatched to Washington to shake the begging bowl on behalf of his country.

Despite his poor health, Keynes tackled these new responsibilities with vigor and panache. The economist Lionel Robbins, who accompanied Keynes to the United States for the American loan negotiations, was dazzled by Keynes' initial performances:

> Keynes must be one of the most remarkable men that have ever lived – the quick logic, the birdlike swoop of intuition, the vivid fancy, the wide vision, above all the incomparable sense of the fitness of words, all combine to make something several degrees beyond the limit of ordinary human achievement ... The Americans sat entranced as the God-like visitor sang and the golden light played round.

Notwithstanding the beatific vision summoned by Robbins, the hard-nosed U.S. contingent remained largely unmoved by this wizardry. Keynes – who, like Churchill, initially had great faith in the purported brotherhood of "the English-speaking peoples" – became increasingly frustrated with what he perceived to be the harsh conditions its putative ally was seeking to impose on Britain.

Keynes remarked of one U.S.-based Treasury colleague that "he could be silent in several languages." Although professing admiration for the eloquent polyglot silence of his workmate, Keynes possessed no such diplomatic reserve. His arguments with the Americans became increasingly heated – Keynes objected to his counterparts "picking out the eyes" of the Empire, while the U.S. contingent was wary of Britain, the cunning Old World fox, whom many Americans believed had "bamboozled" their nation into the Great War and later had the impudence to default on its war loans. James Meade later noted that Keynes and Harry Dexter White, the co-architect of the IMF and the World Bank, would "go for each other in a strident duet of discord which after a crescendo of abuse on either side leads up to a chaotic adjournment."

After the war Keynes' task became, if anything, even more difficult. The Labor Party won a surprise landslide victory over the British bulldog, Winston Churchill, in July 1945, and the United States became even more chary of giving money to a newly socialist government. Under this pressure, Keynes reported that his body gave "ominous signs of conking out." His health was so fragile, in fact, that some German newspapers had published his obituary as early as mid-1944 after news was received that he had suffered another heart attack. As was the case with Mark Twain, reports of Keynes' death were greatly exaggerated. But after making six exhausting trips to the United States to negotiate loans and formulate the structure of a new global monetary scheme, Keynes was fatally weakened. He would not live to see the international monetary system he promoted, the global economic boom his theories forged, nor even the country-saving loan installments he had negotiated.

LAID TO REST

> *Fears and doubts and hypochondriac precautions are keeping us muffled up indoors. But we are not tottering to our graves. We are healthy children. We need the breath of life. There is nothing to be afraid of. On the contrary. The future holds in store for us far more wealth and economic freedom and possibilities of personal life than the past has ever offered.*
>
> —Keynes, *Essays in Persuasion*

On May 2, 1946, a memorial service was held for Keynes in that mausoleum to Old England, Westminster Abbey. Joining Lydia and Keynes' immediate family at the ceremony were representatives from the many different spheres of the man's life – the Prime Minister, Bank of England directors, the Provost and fellows of Eton and King's College, colleagues from the Arts Council, former students, and surviving members of the Bloomsbury group. Keynes' "wonky breathing muscles," laboring under the strain of ceaseless journeys to the United States to simultaneously avert a "financial Dunkirk" and establish a new global monetary body, had finally given out on Easter Sunday. World War II claimed one of its last victims – as Lionel Robbins remarked, Keynes had died "for the cause as certainly as any soldier on the field of battle."

Keynes' life had turned full circle – the prodigal son returned to the heart of a grateful Establishment. The world was utterly unrecognizable from that which had beckoned in the hopeful and carefree days of undergraduate Cambridge and the birth of Bloomsbury. The sun was setting on Britain's Empire, which once proudly shaded a quarter of the world's landmass in imperial pink. The India Office, Keynes' first taste of public service, would be wound up the following year when the subcontinent freed itself from the British Raj. And only a month before Keynes' death, the recently deposed Churchill, on a speaking tour of the

United States, had warned of an "Iron Curtain" descending on Continental Europe. The war-weary world was entering another era, a time of new anxieties and apprehensions.

To untrained eyes, Keynes, too, had changed beyond recognition. The unworldly aesthete had become a rich man and a lord, a promoter of investment companies and an emissary for his country. But this journey from Apostle to apostate was illusory – in many ways, the course of Keynes' life can be seen as an effort to recapture the Edwardian insouciance of his youth, a mythical time when young men lazily punted down the River Cam and discoursed on the finer things in life. Keynes never lost the optimism, the belief in the perfectibility of society, characteristic of that time. "Progress is a soiled creed, black with coal dust and gunpowder; but we have not discarded it," he declared defiantly. Keynes' efforts in the public arena were designed to solve the economic problem so that mankind could "live wisely and agreeably and well." In the personal sphere, too, his moneymaking ventures aimed at the same end – as a means of securing the conditions for a well-lived life, and nothing more.

Keynes substantially achieved what he had preached. He brought confidence and buoyancy to troubled times and, in our field of particular interest, showed that investors could embrace uncertainty rather than be cowed by it. Friedrich von Hayek, who during the war shared with Keynes air-raid warden duties at King's College, wrote that Keynes "was the one really great man I ever knew" – his success as an investor was but a small part of a richly lived life. And his only regret? Some report that, tallying his achievements and disappointments toward the end of his life, Keynes remarked wistfully, "I wish I had drunk more champagne."

NOTES

FURTHER READING

The definitive book for those wishing to examine Keynes' life in greater detail is Robert Skidelsky's *John Maynard Keynes 1883–1946: Economist, Philosopher, Statesman* (2003). Not only does Skidelsky's book provide a comprehensive account of Maynard Keynes' life and ideas, but – due to Keynes' Zelig-like ability to place himself at the heart of so many events of world import – it also offers a fascinating snapshot of Britain in the first half of the twentieth century. A more recent work on Keynes' life, and afterlife as one of the world's most influential "academic scribblers," is Zachary Carter's *The Price of Peace: Money, Democracy, and the Life of John Maynard Keynes* (2020). David Chambers and Elroy Dimson of the Judge Business School, University of Cambridge, provide a comprehensive overview of Keynes' stock market investment performance in "Retrospectives: John Maynard Keynes, Investment Innovator", (*Journal of Economic Perspectives*, 2013), available at https://www.aeaweb.org/articles?id=10.1257/jep.27.3.213; and, together with Justin Foo, in "Keynes the Stock Market Investor: A Quantitative Analysis", (*Journal of Financial and Quantitative Analysis*, 2015), available at https://papers.ssrn.com/sol3/papers.cfm?abstract_id=2023011.

Volume XII of *The Collected Writings of John Maynard Keynes* (1983) is the best general repository of Keynes' opinions on financial exchanges, speculation, and investment. Chapter 12 of *The General Theory of Employment, Interest and Money* (1936) also offers a very readable summary of Keynes' views on the fallibility of stock markets.

There are many books analyzing value investing techniques and, in particular, the stock market strategies of Warren Buffett. Perhaps the best entrée into the world of the Oracle of Omaha lies in Buffett's Chairman's Letters to Berkshire Hathaway stockholders, available online at www.berkshirehathaway.com/letters/letters.html.

RELATIVE MONETARY VALUES

All present-day monetary equivalents are given in U.S. dollars, and have been calculated by reference to the British retail price index series.

REFERENCES

In the notes that follow, *CW* refers to *The Collected Writings of John Maynard Keynes* (variously edited by Donald Moggridge and Elizabeth Johnson), published in thirty volumes between 1971 and 1989 by Palgrave Macmillan for the Royal Economic Society. Catalog references are those of the Archive Centre, King's College, Cambridge, which holds the economic and personal papers of John Maynard Keynes.

*

INTRODUCTION

Page xi *The patient needs exercise* Keynes, J.M., "The Problem of Unemployment – Part II," *The Listener*, January 14, 1931. In a BBC radio broadcast, Keynes asserted: "The patient does not need rest. He needs exercise."

Page xi *so highly regarded by the City* Davenport, J., "Baron Keynes of Tilton," *Fortune*, May 1944

Page xii *the inhabitant of London* Keynes, J.M., *The Economic Consequences of the Peace* (*Collected Writings of John Maynard Keynes* [hereafter *CW*], *Vol. II*), Macmillan, 1919 (1971), p. 6

Page xii *the financial concerns* Letter from J.M. Keynes to the journalist John Davenport, March 21, 1944 (Catalog reference: JMK/A/44/37)

Page xii *brilliance as a practicing investor* Buffett, W., 1991 Chairman's Letter to the shareholders of Berkshire Hathaway Inc., February 28, 1992

Page xiii *exciting literature out of finance* Letter from Lord Beaverbrook to J.M. Keynes, April 18, 1945 (quoted in R. Skidelsky, *John Maynard Keynes: Fighting for Britain 1937–1946* (Volume 3), Macmillan, London, 2000, p. 388)

Page xiii *Practical men, who believe themselves* Keynes, J.M., *The General Theory of Employment, Interest and Money* (*CW, Vol.VII*), 1936, p. 383

Page xiii *row out over that great ocean* Strachey, L., *Eminent Victorians*, Chatto & Windus, London, 1918, p. 7

1: THE APOSTLE MAYNARD

Page 2 *As bursar of his own college* Obituary published in the *Manchester Guardian*, April 22, 1946

Page 2 *such was his influence in the City* Davenport, N., *Memoirs of a City Radical*, Weidenfeld & Nicolson, London, 1974, p. 49

Page 2 *live wisely and agreeably and well* Keynes, J.M., "Economic Possibilities for Our Grandchildren," *Essays in Persuasion (CW, Vol. IX)*, Macmillan, London, 1930 (1972), p. 328

Page 3 *a means to the enjoyment* Ibid.

Page 5 *I should like in certain things* Quoted in D. Moggridge, *Maynard Keynes: An Economist's Biography*, Routledge, London, 1992, p. 35

Page 5 *his hands certainly looked* J.M. Keynes, quoted in R.F. Harrod, *The Life of John Maynard Keynes*, Macmillan, London, 1951, p. 19

Page 5 *dull and soporiferous beyond words* J.M. Keynes, quoted in Moggridge, *Maynard Keynes: An Economist's Biography*, p. 35

Page 5 *the comparative lengths* J.M. Keynes, quoted in Harrod, *The Life of John Maynard Keynes*, p. 29

Page 6 *I've had a good look round* J.M. Keynes, quoted in C.R. Fay, "The Undergraduate," in Keynes, Milo (ed.), *Essays on John Maynard Keynes*, Cambridge University Press, Cambridge, 1975, p. 38

Page 6 *the New Testament is a handbook* Keynes, J.M., "My Early Beliefs," *Two Memoirs (CW, Vol.* X), 1933 (1972), p. 444

Page 6 *By far the most valuable things* Moore, G.E., *Principia Ethica*, Cambridge University Press, Cambridge, 1903, pp. 188–189

Page 6 *we repudiated entirely customary morals* Keynes, J.M., "My Early Beliefs," *Two Memoirs*, p. 446

Page 7 *water-spiders, gracefully skimming* Ibid., p. 450

Page 7 *a metaphysical justification* Beatrice Webb, quoted in G. Himmelfarb, "From Clapham to Bloomsbury: A Genealogy of Morals," *Commentary*, February 1985

Page 7 *I trust your future career* Alfred Marshall, quoted in A. Robinson, "John Maynard Keynes: 1883–1946," *Economic Journal*, Vol. 57, No. 275, March 1947, p. 12

Page 7 *the examiners presumably knew* Ibid.

Page 8 *We found ourselves living* Woolf, L., *Sowing: An Autobiography of the Years 1880 to 1904*, Hogarth Press, London, 1960, pp. 160–161

Page 9 *a gorged seal* Woolf, V., *The Diary of Virginia Woolf: Volume 2, 1920–24*, Penguin, London, 1978 (1981), p. 69

Page 9 *the usual round-up of rootless intellectuals* Buchan, J., *The Island of Sheep*, Wordsworth Editions, Hertfordshire, 1936 (1998), p. 80. Robert Skidelsky (*John Maynard Keynes: Fighting for Britain 1937–1946* (Volume 3), p. 19) notes that the character Joseph Bannatyne Barralty – "half adventurer, half squire" – in *The Island of Sheep* is a thinly disguised portrait of Keynes. In this novel, published the same year as *The General Theory*, Buchan derides Barralty as "the patron of every new fad in painting and sculpting and writing" and refers to Bloomsbury parties where Barralty "was a king among the half-baked." Buchan even furnishes Barralty with a "particular friend" – a "lovely creature" and actress calling herself "Lydia Ludlow." The narrator in *The Island of Sheep* ventures a rationale for Barralty's desire for wealth: "He must have money, great quantities of money, so that he can prove to the world that a fastidious and cynical intellectual can beat the philistines at their own game."

Page 10 *a thesis on mathematics* Obituary published in the *Daily Express*, April 22, 1946

Page 10 *What are you?* Letter from David Garnett to J.M. Keynes, undated (Catalog reference: JMK/PP/45/116/4 and 5)

Page 10 *I should try and come between them* Lytton Strachey, quoted in M. Holroyd, *Lytton Strachey: A Biography*, Penguin, London, 1971, p. 629

Page 10 *absolutely and completely desolated* Letter from J.M. Keynes to Lytton Strachey, November 27, 1914 (quoted in Harrod, *The Life of John Maynard Keynes*, p. 200)

Page 10 *terrible impression for his rudeness* Letter from Basil Blackett to Granville Hamilton, January 1, 1918 (quoted in J.M. Keynes, *The Treasury and Versailles* (*CW, Vol. XVI*), p. 264)
Page 10 *This morning we got a visit* Spring-Rice, C., Papers, Churchill College, Cambridge (quoted in R. Skidelsky, *John Maynard Keynes: Fighting for Britain 1937–1946* (Volume 3), p. 207)
Page 12 *upon there being no causes* Lloyd George, D., "Fontainebleu Memorandum," March 25, 1919
Page 13 *make compensation for all damage* Article 232, Treaty of Versailles, June 28, 1919
Page 13 *The future life of Europe* Keynes, J.M., *The Economic Consequences of the Peace*, p. 35
Page 13 *blind and deaf Don Quixote* Ibid., p. 26
Page 13 *like Odysseus* Ibid., p. 25
Page 13 *one illusion – France* Ibid., p. 20
Page 13 *this goat-footed bard* Keynes, J.M., "Mr. Lloyd George: A Fragment," *Essays in Biography* (*CW, Vol.* X), 1933, p. 23
Page 14 *If we aim deliberately* Keynes, J.M., *The Economic Consequences of the Peace*, p. 170
Page 14 *I woke up like Byron* J.M. Keynes, quoted in J. Davenport, "Baron Keynes of Tilton," *Fortune*, May 1944
Page 14 *Some of this financial decision-making* Hession, C., *John Maynard Keynes*, Macmillan, New York, 1984, p. 175

2: CITIZEN KEYNES

Page 17 *dashed at conclusions with acrobatic ease* Lloyd George, D., *War Memoirs, Volume II*, Ivor Nicholson & Watson, London, 1933, p. 684
Page 18 *the arts of enjoyment* Keynes, J.M., *The Economic Consequences of the Peace*, p. 12
Page 18 *were much in excess* Keynes, J.M., Presidential address to the Society of Apostles, June 21, 1921 (Catalog reference: JMK/66/UA/36)
Page 18 *the stir and bustle of the world* Ibid.
Page 18 *The love of money as a possession* Keynes, J.M., "Economic Possibilities for Our Grandchildren," *Essays in Persuasion*, p. 329
Page 18 *the enjoyments and realities of life* Ibid.
Page 19 *Maynard, who at Cambridge* Bell, C., *Old Friends: Personal Recollections*, Chatto & Windus, London, 1956, pp. 44–45
Page 20 *Money is a funny thing* Letter from J.M. Keynes to Florence Keynes, September 23, 1919 (Catalog reference: JMK/PP/45/168/10/17)
Page 20 *would not look after any private client* Davenport, N., *Memoirs of a City Radical*, p. 44
Page 20 *will shock father* Letter from J.M. Keynes to Florence Keynes, September 3, 1919 (*CW, Vol. XVII*, p. 125)
Page 21 *slaughter of a large part of our holdings* Letter from J.M. Keynes to Vanessa Bell, May 22, 1920 (Catalog reference: CHA/1/341/3/2)
Page 21 *It has been a beastly time* Ibid.
Page 21 *It was perhaps necessary* Letter from Florence Keynes to J.M. Keynes, June 1, 1920 (Catalog reference: JMK/PP/45/168/10/38-9)
Page 21 *quite exhausted my resources* Letter from J.M. Keynes to Sir Ernest Cassel, May 26, 1920 (*CW, Vol. XII*, p. 7)
Page 21 *an unequalled opportunity for speculation* Ibid.
Page 21 *very substantial profits* Ibid.
Page 22 *You must come and see Lady B's ovary* Recounted in Davenport, N., *Memoirs of a City Radical*, p. 47
Page 23 *deafened by the clamorous voices* Keynes, J.M., *The Economic Consequences of Mr. Churchill* (*CW, Vol. IX*), 1925 (1981), p. 212
Page 24 *To debate monetary reform* Letter from J.M. Keynes to *The Times*, March 28, 1925 (*CW, Vol. XIX*, pp. 348–349)

Page 25 *Well-managed industrial companies* Keynes, J.M., "An American Study of Shares Versus Bonds as Permanent Investments," *The Nation and Athenaeum*, May 2, 1925 (*CW, Vol. XII*, p. 250)
Page 26 *the dizzy virtues of compound interest* Keynes, J.M., *The Economic Consequences of the Peace*, p. 13
Page 27 *gold fetters* Keynes, J.M., "The End of the Gold Standard," *Sunday Express*, September 27, 1931 (*CW, Vol. XI*, p. 245)
Page 27 *high tide of prosperity* Keynes, J.M., transcript of CBS broadcast, April 12, 1931 (*CW, Vol.* XX, p. 517)
Page 27 *the most expensive orgy in history* Fitzgerald, F.S., "Echoes of the Jazz Age," *Scribner's Magazine*, Vol. XC, No. 5, 1931, p. 182
Page 28 *I always regard a visit* Letter from J.M. Keynes to P.A.S. Hadley, September 10, 1941 (Catalog reference: JMK/PP/80/9/28)

3: SNAP, OLD MAID, AND MUSICAL CHAIRS

Page 29 *No Congress of the United States* President Calvin Coolidge, State of the Union Address, December 4, 1928
Page 30 *You could talk about Prohibition* Brooks, J., *Once in Golconda*, Allworth Press, New York, 1969 (1997), p. 82
Page 31 *the consensus of judgment of the millions* Lawrence, J.S., *Wall Street and Washington*, Princeton University Press, Princeton, 1929, p. 179
Page 31 *In an efficient market* Fama, E., "Random Walks in Stock Market Prices," *Financial Analysts Journal*, Vol. 21, No. 5, September–October 1965, p. 56
Page 32 *Independence is important* Surowiecki, J., *The Wisdom of Crowds*, Doubleday, New York, 2004, p. 41
Page 34 *If intelligent people* Paul Samuelson, quoted in B. Malkiel, *A Walk Down Wall Street*, Norton, New York, 2003, pp. 196–197
Page 35 *accepted a description of his functions* Eady, W., "Maynard Keynes at the Treasury," *The Listener*, June 7, 1951, p. 920
Page 37 *a peculiar zest in making money quickly* Keynes, J.M., *The General Theory of Employment, Interest and Money (CW, Vol. VII)*, 1936, p. 157
Page 37 *There is nothing so disturbing* Kindleberger, C., *Manias, Panics, and Crashes: A History of Financial Crises*, John Wiley & Sons, New York, 2000, p. 15
Page 38 *The few quiet men* Smiles, S., *The Life of George Stephenson*, John Murray, London, 1881, p. 172
Page 38 *Some artifact or some development* Galbraith, J.K., *A Short History of Financial Euphoria*, Penguin Books, New York, 1993, pp. 2–3
Page 39 *most of these persons* Keynes, J.M., *The General Theory of Employment, Interest and Money*, pp. 154–155
Page 39 *to outwit the crowd* Ibid., p. 155
Page 40 *a game of Snap, of Old Maid* Ibid., pp. 155–156
Page 40 *it may often profit the wisest* Keynes, J.M., *A Treatise on Money – Volume 2:The Applied Theory of Money (CW, Vol.VI)*, 1930 (1971), pp. 323–324
Page 41 *means in practice selling* Letter from J.M. Keynes to R.F. Kahn, May 5, 1938 (*CW, Vol. XII*, p. 100)
Page 41 *a general systematic movement* Memorandum from J.M. Keynes to the Estates Committee, King's College, Cambridge, May 8, 1938 (*CW, Vol. XII*, p. 106)
Page 41 *those newspaper competitions* Keynes, J.M., *The General Theory of Employment, Interest and Money*, p. 156
Page 42 *I want to manage a railway* Letter from J.M. Keynes to Lytton Strachey, November 15, 1905 (Catalogue reference: JMK/PP/45/316/5)
Page 43 *like a weather-vane* Cited in Chancellor, E., *Devil Take the Hindmost*, Macmillan, London, 2000, p. 200

4: THE RECKONING

Page 46 *Sooner or later a crash is coming* Babson, R., *The Commercial and Financial Chronicle*, September 7, 1929 (cited in Galbraith, J.K., *The Great Crash 1929*, Penguin, Middlesex, 1961, p. 108)

Page 46 *Stock prices have reached* For an entertaining account of Irving Fisher's disastrous prognoses, see John Kenneth Galbraith's *The Great Crash 1929*, p. 95, p. 116, and p. 119

Page 47 *for the immediate future at least* Fisher, I., *The Stock Market Crash – and After*, Macmillan, New York, 1930, p. 269

Page 47 *financial storm [has] definitely passed* Cablegram from Bernard Baruch to Winston Churchill, November 15, 1929 (quoted in J. Grant, *Bernard M. Baruch: The Adventures of a Wall Street Legend*, John Wiley & Sons, New York, 1997, p. 227)

Page 49 *commodity prices will recover* Keynes, J.M., "A British View of the Wall Street Slump," *The New York Evening Post*, October 25, 1929 (*CW, Vol.* XX, p. 2)

Page 49 *The fact is – a fact not yet recognized* Keynes, J.M., *The Nation*, May 10, 1930

Page 50 *Some twenty-four thousand families* Heilbroner, R.L., *The Worldly Philosophers: the Great Economic Thinkers*, Allen Lane, London, 1969, p. 242

Page 51 *Activity and boldness and enterprise* Keynes, J.M., "The Problem of Unemployment – Part II," *The Listener*, January 14, 1931

Page 51 *purge the rottenness out of the system* Andrew Mellon, quoted in H. Hoover, *The Memoirs of Herbert Hoover: The Great Depression 1929–1941*, Hollis and Carter, London, 1953, p. 30

Page 51 *an inevitable and a desirable nemesis* Keynes, J.M., "An Economic Analysis of Unemployment," notes for the Harris Foundation lecture, Chicago, June 1931 (*CW, Vol. XIII*, p. 349)

Page 52 *the existing economic system* Keynes, J.M., "Poverty in Plenty: Is the Economic System Self-Adjusting?," *The Listener*, November 21, 1934 (*CW, Vol. XIII*, pp. 486–487)

Page 53 *The modern capitalist* Keynes, J.M., "The World's Economic Outlook," *Atlantic Monthly*, May 1932

Page 53 *a thin and precarious crust* Keynes, J.M., "My Early Beliefs," *Two Memoirs*, p. 447

Page 53 *matters take their natural course* In response to a suggestion by Sir Harry Goschen, Chairman of the National Provincial Bank, that the Government should let "matters take their natural course," Keynes replied tartly: "Is it more appropriate to smile or to rage at these artless sentiments? Best of all, perhaps, just to leave Sir Harry to take his natural course." (Keynes, J.M., "Speeches of the Bank Chairmen," *Nation and Athenaeum*, February 23, 1924 (*CW, Vol. IX*, p. 189))

Page 54 *the enormous anomaly of unemployment* Keynes, J.M., "Economic Possibilities for Our Grandchildren," *Essays in Persuasion*, p. 322

5: RAISING A DUST

Page 55 *out of the tunnel of economic necessity* Keynes, J.M., "Economic Possibilities for Our Grandchildren," *Essays in Persuasion*, p. 331

Page 55 *as humble, competent people* Ibid., p. 332

Page 56 *We shall be able to rid ourselves* Ibid., p. 329

Page 56 *avarice and usury and precaution* Ibid., p. 331

Page 56 *wisely managed, [capitalism] can* Keynes, J.M., "The End of Laissez- Faire" (1926), *Essays in Persuasion*, p. 294

Page 56 *Modern capitalism is absolutely irreligious* Keynes, J.M., "A Short View of Russia" (1925), *Essays in Persuasion*, p. 267

Page 56 *deliver the goods* In a June 1933 article in the *Yale Review*, Keynes noted that:

> "The decadent international but individualistic capitalism in the hands of which we found ourselves after the war is not a success. It is not intelligent. It is not beautiful. It is not just. It is not virtuous. And it doesn't deliver the goods." (Keynes, J.M., "National Self-Sufficiency," *Yale Review*, Vol. 22, No. 4, June 1933)

Page 56 *on a variety of politico-economic experiments* Keynes, J.M., "National Self- Sufficiency," *Yale Review*, Vol. 22, No. 4, June 1933, p. 761

Page 57 *The money changers have fled* President Franklin D. Roosevelt, Inaugural Address, March 4, 1933

Page 59 *complicated hocus-pocus* J.M. Keynes, quoted in M. Straight, *After Long Silence*, Collins, London, 1983, p. 67

Page 59 *as if it were a detective story* Ibid.

Page 59 *was to save the country from me, not to embrace me* Mosley, O., *My Life*, Thomas Nelson & Sons, London, 1968, p. 247

Page 59 *What is prudence in the conduct* Smith, A., *An Enquiry into the Nature and Causes of the Wealth of Nations*, William Pickering, London, 1805 (1995), p. 191

Page 59 *not merely inexpedient, but impious* Keynes, J.M., "The End of Laissez- Faire," *Essays in Persuasion*, p. 276

Page 60 *tacit assumptions are seldom* Keynes, J.M., *The General Theory of Employment, Interest and Money*, p. 378

Page 60 *I am afraid of "principle"* J.M. Keynes, quoted in D. Moggridge, *The Return to Gold*, Cambridge University Press, Cambridge, 1969, p. 90

Page 60 *has ruled over us rather by hereditary right* Keynes, J.M., "The End of Laissez-Faire," *Essays in Persuasion*, p. 287

Page 60 *timidities and mental confusions* Keynes, J.M., "How to Organize a Wave of Prosperity," *The Evening Standard*, July 31, 1928 (*CW, Vol. XIX*, pp. 761–766)

Page 61 *When we have unemployed men* Ibid.

Page 61 *We are ... at one of those uncommon junctures* Keynes, J.M., "Poverty in Plenty: Is the Economic System Self-Adjusting?," *The Listener*, November 21, 1934 (*CW, Vol. XIII*, p. 492)

Page 61 *There is no reason why we should not* Keynes, J.M., "Can Lloyd George Do It?" (1929), *Essays in Persuasion*, p. 125

Page 62 *Euclidean geometers in a non-Euclidean world* Keynes, J.M., *The General Theory of Employment, Interest and Money*, p. 16

Page 62 *largely revolutionize ... the way* Letter from J.M. Keynes to George Bernard Shaw, January 1, 1935 (Catalog reference: JMK/PP/45/291/16; also *CW, Vol. XIII*, pp. 492–493)

Page 63 *vain and insatiable desires* Smith, A., *The Theory of Moral Sentiments*, Cambridge University Press, Cambridge, 1759 (2002), p. 215

Page 63 *Keynes and all his school* Letter from Russell Leffingwell to Walter Lippmann, December 30, 1931 (quoted in R. Skidelsky, *John Maynard Keynes: The Economist as Savior 1920–1937* (Volume 2), Macmillan, London, 1992, pp. 398–399)

Page 64 *none of the wheels of trade* Hume, D., "Of Money", reprinted in *Essays: Moral, Political and Literary*, Cosimo Classics, New York, 1754 (2006), p. 289

Page 64 *above all, a subtle device for linking* Keynes, J.M., *The General Theory of Employment, Interest and Money*, p. 294

Page 64 *our desire to hold Money* Keynes, J.M., "The General Theory of Employment," *The Quarterly Journal of Economics*, Vol. 51, No. 2, February 1937, p. 216 (see also *CW, Vol. XIV*, p. 116)

Page 64 *enterprise will fade and die* Keynes, J.M., *The General Theory of Employment, Interest and Money*, p. 162

Page 65 *we are suffering from the growing pains* Keynes, J.M., "The Problem of Unemployment," BBC symposium, January 12, 1931 (Catalog reference: JMK/BR/1/121)

Page 65 *The important thing for government* Keynes, J.M., "The End of Laissez- Faire," *Essays in Persuasion*, p. 291

Page 66 *a farrago of confused sophistication* Letter from Hubert Henderson to Roy Harrod, April 2, 1936 (quoted in D. Besomi (ed.), *The Collected Interwar Papers and Correspondence of Roy Harrod, Volume II: Correspondence, 1936–39*, Edward Elgar Publishing, Cheltenham, p. 540)

Page 66 *We have watched an artist firing arrows* Pigou, A., "Mr. J.M. Keynes' General Theory of Employment, Interest and Money," *Economica*, Vol. 3, No. 10, May 1936, p. 132

Page 66 *the pessimism of the reactionaries* Keynes, J.M., "Economic Possibilities for Our Grandchildren," *Essays in Persuasion*, p. 322

Page 66 *moderately conservative in its implications* Keynes, J.M., *The General Theory of Employment, Interest and Money*, p. 377

Page 66 *our central controls succeed* Ibid., p. 378

Page 67 *We are all Keynesians now* Milton Friedman, quoted in "We Are All Keynesians Now," *Time*, December 31, 1965

6: ANIMAL SPIRITS

Page 69 *Nature and Nature's laws* Alexander Pope, "Epitaph for Sir Isaac Newton" (1727)

Page 70 *the grand secret of the whole Machine* John Arbuthnot, *An Essay on the Usefulness of Mathematical Learning* (1745)

Page 70 *chemical experiments ... aimed at something* Letter from Humphrey Newton to John Conduitt, January 17, 1727 (quoted in J.M. Keynes, "Bernard Shaw and Isaac Newton," *Essays in Biography*, p. 377)

Page 70 *whim or sentiment or chance* Keynes, J.M., *The General Theory of Employment, Interest and Money*, p. 163

Page 70 *purely irrational waves of optimism or depression* Keynes, J.M., "Great Britain's Foreign Investments," *New Quarterly*, February 1910 (*CW, Vol. XV*, p. 46)

Page 71 *one foot in the Middle Ages* Keynes, J.M., "Newton, the Man," *Essays in Biography*, p. 370

Page 71 *there is no scientific basis* Keynes, J.M., "The General Theory of Employment," *Economica*, p. 214 (see also *CW, Vol. XIV*, p. 114)

Page 71 *The outstanding fact is the extreme* Keynes, J.M., *The General Theory of Employment, Interest and Money*, pp. 149–150

Page 72 *Wishes are fathers to thoughts* Keynes, J.M., "An Economic Analysis of Unemployment" (*CW, Vol. XIII*, p. 343)

Page 72 *a good Benthamite calculation* Keynes, J.M., "The General Theory of Employment," *Economica*, p. 214 (see also *CW, Vol. XIV*, p. 114)

Page 72 *we simply do not know* Ibid.

Page 72 *the necessity for action and for decision* Ibid.

Page 73 *To avoid being in the position of Buridan's ass* Letter from J.M. Keynes to Hugh Townsend, December 7, 1938, in *The General Theory and After: A Supplement* (*CW, Vol. XXIX*), p. 294

Page 73 *spontaneous urge to action rather than inaction* Keynes, J.M., *The General Theory of Employment, Interest and Money*, p. 161

Page 73 *a large proportion of our positive activities* Ibid.

Page 74 *how sensitive – over-sensitive if you like* Keynes, J.M., *Treatise on Money – Volume 2*, p. 322

Page 74 *even though they may be less* Keynes, J.M., *The General Theory of Employment, Interest and Money*, p. 148

Page 74 *the facts of the existing situation* Ibid.

Page 75 *the existing state of affairs* Ibid., p. 152

Page 75 *Day-to-day fluctuations* Ibid., pp. 153–154

Page 75 *the shares of American companies* Ibid., p. 154

Page 75 *recurrence of a bank-holiday may raise* Ibid.

Page 75 *Faced with the perplexities and uncertainties* Speech by J.M. Keynes to the Annual Meeting of the National Mutual Life Assurance Society, February 23, 1938 (*CW, Vol. XXI*, p. 445)

Page 76 *all sorts of considerations* Keynes, J.M., *The General Theory of Employment, Interest and Money*, p. 152

Page 76 *made many ruinous investments* White, E., *Proust*, Weidenfeld & Nicolson, London, 1999, pp. 84–85

Page 77 *investors are unromantically concerned* Brealey, R., and Myers, S., *Principles of Corporate Finance*, McGraw-Hill, New York, 1981, p. 266

Page 77 *The atomic hypothesis that has worked* Keynes, J.M., "Francis Ysidro Edgeworth, 1845–1926," *The Economic Journal*, March 1926 (*CW, Vol.* X, p. 262)

Page 77 *We are faced at every turn* Ibid.

Page 79 *I can only say that I was the principal inventor* Letter from J.M. Keynes to R.F. Kahn, May 5, 1938 (*CW, Vol. XII*, p. 100)

Page 79 *phenomenal skill to make much out of it* Ibid.

Page 79 *I am clear that the idea of wholesale* Memorandum from J.M. Keynes to the Estates Committee, King's College, Cambridge, May 5, 1938 (*CW, Vol. XII*, p. 106)

7: GAME PLAYERS

Page 81 *Nobles, citizens, farmers* Mackay, C., *Extraordinary Popular Delusions and the Madness of Crowds*, Wordsworth, Hertfordshire, 1841 (1995), p. 94

Page 82 *When it has been weakened by cultivation* Ibid., p. 90

Page 82 *the organization of investment markets* Keynes, J.M., *The General Theory of Employment, Interest and Money*, p. 158

Page 83 *so much in the minority* Ibid., p. 150

Page 83 *That the sins of the London Stock Exchange* Ibid., p. 159

Page 83 *have no special knowledge* Ibid., p. 153

Page 84 *since there will be no strong roots* Ibid., p. 154

Page 84 *a frequent opportunity to the individual* Ibid., p. 151

Page 84 *an abstraction, a name, a symbol* Herbert, Z., "The Bitter Smell of Tulips," in *Still Life with a Bridle*, The Ecco Press, Hopewell, New Jersey, 1993, p. 47

Page 85 *It might have been supposed* Keynes, J.M., *The General Theory of Employment, Interest and Money*, p. 154

Page 86 *it is the long-term investor* Ibid., pp. 157–158

Page 87 *price fluctuations have only one* Graham, B., *The Intelligent Investor*, Collins, New York, 2003, p. 205

Page 88 *is very obliging indeed* Ibid.

Page 88 *lets his enthusiasm or his fears* Ibid.

Page 89 *We've seen oil magnates* Rothchild, J., "How Smart is Warren Buffett?," *Time*, April 3, 1995

Page 90 *various forms of mass hysteria* Warren Buffett, quoted in J. Lowe, *Warren Buffett Speaks*, John Wiley & Sons, New York, 1997, p. 114

Page 90 *began as a market-timer* Buffett, W., 1988 Chairman's Letter, February 28, 1989

Page 91 *the activity of forecasting the psychology* Keynes, J.M., *The General Theory of Employment, Interest and Money*, p. 158

Page 91 *forecasting the prospective yield* Ibid.

Page 91 *assumes the ability to pick specialties* Letter from J.M. Keynes to R.F. Kahn, May 5, 1938 (*CW, Vol. XII*, pp. 100–101)

Page 92 *demi-semi-official* Quoted in Moggridge, *Maynard Keynes: An Economist's Biography*, p. 118

8: SEARCHING FOR STUNNERS

Page 96 *ventured some of his money* Johnson, S., "The Life of Pope," in *Lives of the Poets, Volume III*, John Henry and James Parker, Oxford and London, 1781 (1865), p. 49

Page 97 *Every mortal that has common sense* Sarah, Duchess of Marlborough, quoted in M. Balen, *A Very English Deceit: The Secret History of the South Sea Bubble and the First Great Financial Scandal*, Fourth Estate, London, 2002, p. 119

Page 97 *almost repellent common sense* Chancellor, E., *Devil Take the Hindmost*, Macmillan, London, 2000, p. 80 (n.)

Page 97 *the laws of arithmetic were more reliable* Harrod, *The Life of John Maynard Keynes*, p. 302

Page 98 *inordinate thirst of gain that had afflicted* Mackay, *Extraordinary Popular Delusions and the Madness of Crowds*, p. 52

Page 98 *for carrying on an undertaking* Ibid., p. 55

Page 98 *cold and untinctured reason* Keynes, J.M., "Newton, the Man," *Essays in Biography*, p. 363

Page 98 *unwholesome fermentation* Mackay, *Extraordinary Popular Delusions and the Madness of Crowds*, p. 71

Page 98 *the hope of boundless wealth* Ibid.

Page 99 *his unusual powers of continuous concentrated introspection* Keynes, J.M., "Newton, the Man," *Essays in Biography*, p. 364

Page 100 *In an efficient market you can trust* Brealey and Myers, *Principles of Corporate Finance*, p. 264

Page 100 *With the growing optimism* Hoover, *The Memoirs of Herbert Hoover: The Great Depression 1929–1941*, p. 5

Page 101 *Observing correctly that the market* Buffett, W., 1988 Chairman's Letter, February 28, 1989

Page 101 *when the safety, excellence and cheapness* Letter from J.M. Keynes to F.C. Scott, February 6, 1942 (*CW, Vol. XII*, p. 82)

Page 102 *the market is not a weighing machine* Graham, B. and Dodd, D., *Security Analysis*, McGraw-Hill, New York, 1940 (2005), p. 28

Page 102 *The market may ignore business success* Buffett, W., 1987 Chairman's Letter, February 29,1988

Page 102 *The fact is that when the perception* Bogle, J., "Don't Count On It! The Perils of Numeracy," address to Princeton University, October 18, 2002

Page 103 *For the seriously long-term investor* Dimson, E., Marsh, P., and Staunton, M., *ABN Amro Global Investment Returns Yearbook 2005*, p. 36. Note also that in John Bogle's October 2002 address, referred to above, he provides further evidence to support the argument that markets are efficient in the long run:

> "it is an irrefutable fact that in the long run it is economics that triumphs over emotion. Since 1872, the average annual real stock market return (after inflation but before intermediation costs) has been 6.5%. The *real* investment return generated by dividends and earnings growth has come to 6.6% ... Speculative return slashed *investment* return by more than one-half during the 1970s and then *tripled*(!) it during the 1980s and 1990s. But measured today, after this year's staggering drop in stock prices, *speculative* return, with a *net* negative annual return of –0.1% during the entire 130-year period, on balance neither contributed to, nor materially detracted from, investment return."

Page 103 *search for discrepancies between* Buffett, W., "The Superinvestors of Graham-and-Doddsville," *Hermes* (magazine of the Columbia Business School), Fall 1984

Page 104 *My purpose is to buy securities* Letter from J.M. Keynes to F.C. Scott, February 6, 1942 (*CW, Vol. XII*, p. 82)

Page 105 *Speculative markets ... are governed* Speech by J.M. Keynes at the Annual Meeting of National Mutual Life Assurance Society, February 23, 1938 (*CW, Vol. XII*, p. 238)

Page 106 *loved a bargain* Bell, *Old Friends: Personal Recollections*, p. 52

Page 106 *eyes gleamed as the bones went round* Virginia Woolf, quoted in R. Skidelsky, *John Maynard Keynes 1883–1946: Economist, Philosopher, Statesman*, Macmillan, London, 2003, p. 362

Page 106 *intrinsic values ... enormously in excess* Letter from J.M. Keynes to F.C. Scott, April 10, 1940 (*CW, Vol. XII*, p. 77)

Page 107 *It is a much safer and easier way* Letter from J.M. Keynes to R.F. Kahn, May 5, 1938 (*CW, Vol. XII*, p. 101)

9: SAFETY FIRST

Page 110 *where the fall in value* Letter from J.M. Keynes to F.C. Scott, June 7, 1938 (*CW, Vol. XII*, p. 66)
Page 111 *amalgam of logic and intuition* Keynes, J.M., *Essays in Biography*, p. 186, *n.* 2
Page 111 *in the study of such complex* von Hayek, F., "The Pretence of Knowledge," Nobel Prize Lecture, December 11, 1974
Page 111 *cannot be confirmed by quantitative evidence* Ibid.
Page 111 *they thereupon happily proceed* Ibid.
Page 112 *When statistics do not seem to* Letter from J.M. Keynes to E. Rothbarth, January 21, 1940 (Catalog reference: JMK/W/4/69)
Page 112 *To the man with only a hammer* Charles Munger, quoted in "A Lesson on Elementary Worldly Wisdom As It Relates to Investment Management & Business," *Outstanding Investor Digest*, May 5, 1995, p. 49
Page 112 *practically everybody (1) overweighs* Munger, C., "Academic Economics: Strengths and Faults After Considering Interdisciplinary Needs," Herb Kay Undergraduate Lecture, University of California, Santa Barbara, October 3, 2003
Page 112 *It seems that the immature mind* Schwed, F., *Where Are the Customers' Yachts?*, John Wiley & Sons, New York, 1940 (1995), p. 19
Page 113 *peace and comfort of mind require* Keynes, J.M., *The General Theory and After: Part II* (*CW, Vol. XIV*), 1937 (1973), p. 124
Page 113 *institutional investors do not feel* Shiller, R., "Bubbles, Human Judgment and Expert Opinion," Yale International Center for Finance, February 5, 2001
Page 114 *The combination of precise formulas* Graham, *The Intelligent Investor,* pp. 564, 570
Page 114 *readers limit themselves to issues* Graham, *The Intelligent Investor,* p. 9
Page 116 *It's exactly what I would do* Buffett, B., transcript of a meeting of the New York Society of Financial Analysts, December 6, 1994
Page 116 *a number that is impossible to pinpoint* Buffett, W., 1994 Chairman's Letter, March 7, 1995
Page 116 *seen dependable calculations* Graham, *The Intelligent Investor*, p. 570
Page 117 *Just as Justice Stewart found it* Buffett, W., 1993 Chairman's Letter, March 1, 1994
Page 117 *for absorbing the effect of miscalculations* Graham, *The Intelligent Investor*, p. 518
Page 117 *To use a homely simile* Graham and Dodd, *Security Analysis*, p. 22
Page 118 *Speculation is an effort, probably unsuccessful* Schwed, *Where Are the Customers' Yachts?*, p. 172
Page 118 *the thought of ultimate loss* Keynes, J.M., *The General Theory of Employment, Interest and Money*, p. 162
Page 118 *It will be remembered that the seventy* Keynes, J.M., Review on "A Method and its Application to Investment Activity," *Economic Journal*, March 1940 (*CW, Vol. XIV*, p. 320)
Page 118 *there is no place where the calculations* Walter Bagehot, quoted in J.M. Keynes, "The Works of Bagehot," *The Economic Journal*, Vol. 25, No. 19, September 1915, p. 373
Page 119 *the amount of the risk to any investor* Keynes, J.M., "Great Britain's Foreign Investments," *New Quarterly*, February 1910 (*CW, Vol. XV*, p. 46)
Page 119 *there are many individual investments* Keynes, J.M., *The General Theory of Employment, Interest and Money*, p. 163
Page 119 *the more uncertain the future* Buffett, W., 2005 Chairman's Letter, February 28, 2006
Page 120 *See's was ... then annually earning* Buffett, W., 2014 Chairman's Letter, February 28, 2015
Page 121 *Our power of prediction is so slight* Keynes, J.M., "The Political Doctrines of Edmund Burke" (1904) (Catalog reference: JMK/ UA/20/14)
Page 121 *demonstrated consistent earning power*, Buffett,W., 1982 Chairman's Letter, March 3, 1983
Page 121 *Economics is essentially a moral science* Letter from J.M. Keynes to Roy Harrod, July 4, 1938 (quoted in Besomi, *The Collected Interwar Papers and Correspondence of Roy Harrod, Volume II*, p. 796)

Page 122 *Valuing a business is part art and part science* Warren Buffett, quoted in A. Smith, "The Modest Billionaire," *Esquire*, October 1988, p. 103

Page 122 *You also have to have the knowledge* Buffett, W., "The Superinvestors of Graham-and-Doddsville," *Hermes*, Fall 1984

10: LEANING INTO THE WIND

Page 126 *your existence at the Treasury* Letter from Vanessa Bell to J.M. Keynes, March 23, 1918 (quoted in Harrod, *The Life of John Maynard Keynes*, p. 226)

Page 127 *all the common-or-garden thoughts* MacKenzie, N. and MacKenzie, J. (eds), *The Diary of Beatrice Webb, Volume 4: 1924–1943, The Wheel of Life*, Virago, London, 1985, p. 94

Page 128 *Those classes of investments* Schwed, *Where Are the Customers' Yachts?*, p. 102

Page 128 *The market is fond of making mountains* Graham, *The Intelligent Investor*, p. 167

Page 129 *what we have created at Berkshire* Charles Munger, quoted in J. Lowe, *Damn Right! Behind the Scenes with Berkshire Hathaway Billionaire Charlie Munger*, John Wiley & Sons, New York, 2000, p. 162

Page 130 *What the few bought for the right reason* Buffett and Loomis, "Warren Buffett on the Stock Market," *Fortune*, December 10, 2001

Page 131 *Everybody goes [to the racetrack] and bets* Munger, C., "A Lesson on Elementary Worldly Wisdom As It Relates to Investment Management & Business," *Outstanding Investor Digest*, May 5, 1995, p. 57

Page 131 *to understand the odds* Charles Munger, quoted in "In the Money," *Harvard Law Bulletin*, Summer 2001

Page 132 *Were it possible for anyone* Galbraith, J. K., *A History of Economics: The Past as Present*, Penguin, London, 1989, p. 4

Page 132 *The art of investing, if there is such* Letter from J.M. Keynes to F.C. Scott, April 1944 (Catalog reference: JMK/PC/1/9/295)

Page 133 *It is because particular individuals* Keynes, J.M., "The End of Laissez- Faire," *Essays in Persuasion*, p. 291

Page 134 *many [investors who expect to be net buyers]* Buffett,W., 1990 Chairman's Letter, March 1, 1991

Page 134 *Very few American investors* Letter from J.M. Keynes to F.C. Scott, April 10, 1940 (*CW, Vol. XII*, p. 78)

Page 135 *The odds appear to me* slightly *against* Letter from J.M. Keynes to his father, John Neville Keynes, July 28, 1914 (Catalogue reference: JMK/PP/45/168/7/244)

Page 136 *[Berkshire Hathaway] made over half* Buffett. W., transcript of a lecture to Notre Dame faculty, Spring 1991

Page 137 *the importance of being in businesses* Buffett, W., 1977 Chairman's Letter, March 14, 1978

Page 117 *great companies with dominant positions* Warren Buffett, quoted in Lowe, *Warren Buffett Speaks*, p. 146

Page 137 *It is generally a good rule* Keynes, J.M., *The Nation and Athenaeum*, June 2, 1923 (*CW, Vol. XIX*, p. 93)

Page 138 *Over the long term, it's hard* Charles Munger, quoted in "A Lesson on Elementary Worldly Wisdom As It Relates to Investment Management & Business," *Outstanding Investor Digest*, May 5, 1995

Page 139 *ten-year real returns* Schiller, R., "Bubbles, Human Judgment, and Expert Opinion," Cowles Foundation Discussion Paper, May 2001

Page 139 *a strategy of buying extreme losers* De Bondt, W., and Thaler, R., "Financial Decision-Making in Markets and Firms: A Behavioural Perspective," in R. Jarrow, V. Maksimovic, and W. Ziemba, *Handbook in Operational Research and Management Science*, Elsevier Science, Amsterdam, 1995, p. 394

Page 140 *By all means, but timing is important* J.M. Keynes, quoted in D. Moggridge (ed.), *Economic Articles and Correspondence: Investment and Editorial (CW, Vol. XII)*, 1983, p. 50
Page 141 *now hopelessly out of fashion* Letter from J.M. Keynes to F. C. Scott, November 23, 1933 (*CW, Vol. XII*, p. 61)
Page 141 *some of the American preferred stocks* Ibid.
Page 141 *In '74 you could have bought* Buffett, W., transcript of lecture to Notre Dame students, 1991
Page 142 *Fear is the foe of the faddist* Buffett, W., 1994 Chairman's Letter, March 7, 1995
Page 142 *fluttering dovecotes, particularly in the City* Obituary published in *The Daily Express*, April 22, 1946
Page 142 *Tammany Polonius* Letter from J.M. Keynes to Sir John Anderson, December 12, 1944 (*CW, Vol. XXIV*, p. 218)
Page 142 *ear [was] so near* Ibid., p. 204
Page 142 *the buttocks of a baboon* J.M. Keynes, quoted in Moggridge, *Maynard Keynes: An Economist's Biography*, p. 799
Page 142 No *wonder that man is a Mormon* J.M. Keynes, quoted in Skidelsky, *John Maynard Keynes: Fighting for Britain* (Volume 3), p. 435
Page 143 *a menace in international negotiations* Howson, S., and Moggridge, D. (eds), *The Wartime Diaries of Lionel Robbins and James Meade*, Palgrave Macmillan, Basingstoke, 1990, p. 122
Page 143 *My central principle of investment* Letter from J.M. Keynes to Sir Jasper Ridley, March 1944 (*CW, Vol. XII*, p. 111)
Page 143 *(1) inherently sound and promising, and* Graham, *The Intelligent Investor*, p. 31
Page 143 *extraordinary business franchises with* Buffett,W., 1980 Chairman's Letter, February 27, 1981

11: BEING QUIET

Page 145 *glorious work of fine intelligence* William Wordsworth, "Within King's College Chapel, Cambridge" (1825)
Page 146 *"Be Quiet" is our best motto* Memorandum from J.M. Keynes to the National Mutual Life Assurance board, February 18, 1931 (*CW, Vol. XII*, p. 19)
Page 147 *there is no moral difference* President Theodore Roosevelt, Annual Message to Congress, January 31, 1908, 42 Congressional Record, p. 1349
Page 147 *it is much better that gambling* J.M. Keynes, quoted in the minutes of evidence of the Royal Commission on Lotteries and Betting, December 15, 1932 (*CW, Vol. XXVIII*, p. 406)
Page 147 *the whole of [a nation's] industry* Ibid., p. 399
Page 147 *Where risk is unavoidably present* Keynes, J.M., *A Tract on Monetary Reform (CW, Vol. IV)*, 1923, p. 136
Page 148 *proper social purpose is to direct* Keynes, J.M., *The General Theory of Employment, Interest and Money*, p. 159
Page 148 *is largely a matter of A trying to decide* Graham and Dodd, *Security Analysis*, p. 443
Page 148 *The social object of skilled investment* Keynes, J.M., *The General Theory of Employment, Interest and Money*, p. 155
Page 149 *a somewhat comprehensive socialization* Ibid., p. 378
Page 150 *powerful operation of compound interest* Keynes, J.M., *The Economic Consequences of the Peace*, p. 126, *n.* 1
Page 150 *how long will it be found necessary* Keynes, J.M., *Indian Currency and Finance (CW, Vol. I)*, 1913 (1971), p. 51
Page 150 *After all one would expect brokers* Letter from J.M. Keynes to David Hill, February 1, 1944 (Catalog reference: JMK/PP/45/143/2)
Page 150 *Wall Street is the only place* Warren Buffett, quoted in Lowe, *Warren Buffett Speaks*, p. 114
Page 151 *I join John Maynard Keynes* Comments by Charlie Munger at the 2005 Berkshire Hathaway Annual Meeting

Page 151 *Never ask a barber if you need a haircut* Warren Buffett, quoted in Lowe, *Warren Buffett Speaks*, p. 112

Page 152 *self-inflicted wounds* Buffett, W., 2005 Chairman's Letter, February 28, 2006

Page 152 *hyperactive stock market is the pickpocket* Buffett, W., 1983 Chairman's Letter, March 14, 1984

Page 152 *There are* huge *advantages* Munger, C., *Outstanding Investor Digest*, May 5, 1995

Page 153 *For investors as a whole* Buffett, W., 2005 Chairman's Letter, February 28, 2006

Page 153 *human nature desires quick results* Keynes, J.M., *The General Theory of Employment, Interest and Money*, p. 157

Page 153 *The introduction of a substantial* Ibid., p. 160

Page 154 *to make the purchase of an investment* Ibid.

Page 154 *our 'til-death-do-us-part policy* Buffett, W., 1986 Chairman's Letter, February 27, 1987

Page 154 *determination to have and to hold* Buffett, W., 1987 Chairman's Letter, February 29, 1988

12: EGGS IN ONE BASKET

Page 155 *embark[ing] money and strength* Cited in R. Skidelsky, *John Maynard Keynes: Hopes Betrayed, 1883–1920* (*Volume 1*), Macmillan, London, 1983, p. 5

Page 156 *Sorry to have gone too large* Letter from J.M. Keynes to F.C. Scott, February 6, 1942 (*CW, Vol. XII*, p. 79)

Page 157 *scattering one's investments* Letter from J.M. Keynes to F.C. Scott, February 1945 (Catalog reference: JMK/PC/1/9/366)

Page 157 *Diversification serves as protection* Comments by Warren Buffett at the 1996 Berkshire Hathaway Annual Meeting

Page 158 *it ought to be considered as imprudent* Speech by J.M. Keynes at the National Mutual Life Assurance Society annual meeting, January 29, 1923 (*CW, Vol. XII*, p. 125)

Page 158 *both own a large number of equities* Buffett, W., 1993 Chairman's Letter, March 1, 1994

Page 159 *it is out of these big units* Letter from J.M. Keynes to F.C. Scott, April 10, 1940 (*CW, Vol. XII*, p. 78)

Page 159 *the important thing is that when you do* Comments by Warren Buffett at the 1998 Berkshire Hathaway Annual Meeting

Page 159 *If something is not worth doing at all* Buffett, W., 1994 Chairman's Letter, March 7, 1995

Page 159 *I cannot understand why* Buffett, W., 1993 Chairman's Letter, March 1,1994

Page 160 *is an admission of not knowing* Loeb, G., *The Battle for Investment Survival*, Wiley, New York, 1935 (1996), p. 119

Page 160 *Send your grain across the seas* Ecclesiastes 11:1–2

Page 161 *my theory of risk* Letter from J.M. Keynes to F.C. Scott, February 1945 (Catalog reference: JMK/PC/1/9/366)

Page 161 *one investment about which* Letter from J.M. Keynes to F.C. Scott, February 6, 1942 (*CW, Vol. XII*, p. 81)

Page 161 *I play for small stakes* David Ricardo, quoted in P. Sraffa (ed.), *The Works and Correspondence of David Ricardo: Biographical Miscellany, Volume* X, Cambridge University Press, Cambridge, 1955, p. 81

Page 162 *When you got nothing, you got nothing to lose* Bob Dylan, "Like a Rolling Stone," *Highway 61 Revisited*, Copyright © 1965; renewed 1993 Special Rider Music

Page 162 *both the intensity with which* Buffett, W., 1993 Chairman's Letter, March 1, 1994

Page 163 *false to believe that one* Keynes, J.M., "Foreword to *King Street, Cheapside* by G. H. Recknell," (*CW, Vol. XII*), 1936, p. 243

Page 163 *practical investors usually learn* Fisher, P., *Common Stocks and Uncommon Profits*, John Wiley & Sons, New York, 1958 (1996), p. 117

Page 164 *there are seldom more than two or three* Letter from J.M. Keynes to F.C. Scott, August 15, 1934 (*CW, Vol. XII*, p. 57)

Page 164 *Playing poker in the Army* Charles Munger, quoted in Lowe, *Damn Right! Behind the Scenes with Berkshire Hathaway Billionaire Charlie Munger*, p. 36

Page 165 *To suggest that this investor* Buffett, W., 1996 Chairman's Letter, February 28, 1997

Page 165 *investors have a tendency to sell assets* see, for example, Kahneman, D., *Thinking, Fast and Slow*, Penguin Books, 2011, p. 344

Page 166 *the right investment policy for [the Society]* Keynes, J.M., quoted in N. Davenport, "Keynes in the City," in *Essays on John Maynard Keynes*, p. 225

Page 166 *ought not to be carried too far* Letter from J.M. Keynes to F.C. Scott, August 15, 1934 (*CW, Vol. XII*, p. 57)

Page 166 *a variety of risks in spite of* Memorandum from J.M. Keynes to the Estates Committee, King's College, Cambridge, May 8, 1938 (*CW, Vol. XII*, p. 107)

Page 168 *five to ten sensibly-priced companies* Buffett, W., 1993 Chairman's Letter, March 1, 1994

Page 168 *To carry one's eggs in a great* Memorandum from J.M. Keynes to the Provincial Insurance Company, March 7, 1938 (*CW, Vol. XII*, p. 99)

Page 168 *As time goes on I get more* Letter from J.M. Keynes to F. C. Scott, August 15, 1934 (*CW, Vol. XII*, p. 57)

13: A SENSE OF PROPORTION

Page 171 *strenuous purposeful moneymakers* Keynes, J.M., "Economic Possibilities for Our Grandchildren," *Essays in Persuasion*, p. 328

Page 171 *dangerous human proclivities can be canalized* Keynes, J.M., *The General Theory of Employment, Interest and Money*, p. 374

Page 172 *The thing is good as a means* Letter from J.M. Keynes to Duncan Grant, January 22, 1909 (see Skidelsky, *John Maynard Keynes: Hopes Betrayed 1883–1920 (Volume 1)*, p. 202)

Page 172 *It is not easy, it seems, for men* Keynes, J.M., *A Tract on Monetary Reform (CW, Vol. IX*, p. 170)

Page 173 *a sound intellectual framework* Buffett, W., Preface to Graham, *The Intelligent Investor*, p. ix

Page 173 *sad lot with drawn, dejected faces* Keynes, J.M., "Dr Melchior: A Defeated Enemy," *Two Memoirs*, p. 395

Page 173 *brilliant and engaging personality* Speech by J.M. Keynes at the National Mutual Life Assurance Annual Meeting, January 20, 1931 (*CW, Vol. XII*, p. 178)

Page 173 *as much equanimity and patience* Memorandum from J.M. Keynes to the Estates Committee, King's College, Cambridge, May 8, 1938 (*CW, Vol. XII*, p. 108)

Page 173 *much more willing to run a risk* Keynes, J.M., *The General Theory of Employment, Interest and Money*, p. 160

Page 174 *One must not allow one's attitude* Memorandum from J.M. Keynes to the Estates Committee, King's College, Cambridge, May 8, 1938 (*CW, Vol. XII*, p. 108)

Page 174 *robust faith in the ultimate rightness* Letter from F.C. Scott to J.M. Keynes, January 1939 (*CW, Vol. XII*, p. 50)

Page 174 *[g]ames are won by players who focus on* Buffett, W., 2013 Chairman's Letter, March 28, 2014

Page 174 *Buying a neglected and therefore* Graham, *The Intelligent Investor*, p. 32

Page 175 *I do not draw from this conclusion* Memorandum from J.M. Keynes to the National Mutual Life Assurance board, February 18, 1931 (*CW, Vol. XII*, p. 18)

Page 175 *a certain continuity of policy* Letter from J.M. Keynes to F.C. Scott, November 29, 1933 (*CW, Vol. XII*, p. 65)

Page 175 *it seems to me to be most important* Letter from J.M. Keynes to F.C. Scott, August 23, 1934 (*CW, Vol. XII*, pp. 58–59)

Page 176 *disposition to own stocks without fretting* Comments by Charles Munger at the 2003 Berkshire Hathaway Annual Meeting

Page 176 *The inactive investor who takes up* Keynes, J.M., "Investment Policy for Insurance Companies," *The Nation and Athenaeum*, May 17, 1924 (*CW, Vol. XII*, p. 243)

Page 177 *constant vigilance, constant revision* Ibid., p. 244

Page 177 *The great point about King's* Report by Ministry of Agriculture officials, December 18, 1926 (quoted in Moggridge, *Maynard Keynes: An Economist's Biography*, p. 411)

Page 177 *I have never known a man so quick* Davenport, N., *Memoirs of a City Radical*, p. 50

Page 179 *You only find out who is swimming* Buffett, W., 2001 Chairman's Letter, February 28, 2002

Page 179 *an investor who proposes* Keynes, J.M., *The General Theory of Employment, Interest and Money*, p. 157

Page 179 *chicken about buying stocks on margin* Charles Munger, quoted in R. Lenzner, and D.S. Fondiller, "Meet Charlie Munger," *Forbes*, January 22, 1996

Page 179 *The ideal is to borrow in a way* Ibid.

Page 180 *Investing is not a game where* Warren Buffett, quoted in an interview with *BusinessWeek*, June 25, 1999

Page 180 *good business judgment with an ability* Buffett, W., 1987 Chairman's Letter, February 29, 1988

Page 180 *The overweening conceit which the greater* Smith, A., *An Inquiry into the Nature and Causes of the Wealth of Nations*, Volume 1, p. 168

Page 180 *The stock doesn't know you own it* Lecture by Warren Buffett to the University of Florida School of Business, October 15, 1998

Page 181 *a great big casino … [where] everyone else is boozing* Warren Buffett, quoted in an interview with *Forbes*, November 1, 1972

Page 181 *rather in the nature of a family affair* Letter from J.M. Keynes to John Davenport, March 21, 1944 (Catalog reference: JMK/A/44/37)

Page 182 *It is remarkable how much long-term* Munger, C., Wesco Financial Corporation Annual Report, 1989

Page 183 *their brains make them dangerous* Quoted in *Fortune* magazine, September 1933 (cited by Skidelsky, *John Maynard Keynes 1883–1946: Economist, Philosopher, Statesman*, p. 961)

Page 183 *much patience and courage* Letter from J.M. Keynes to G.H. Recknell, January 19, 1939 (*CW, Vol. XII*, p.49)

Page 183 *the investor's chief problem* Graham, *The Intelligent Investor*, p. 8

Page 184 *more temperament than logic* Letter from J.M. Keynes to Richard Kahn, May 5, 1938 (*CW, Vol. XII*, p. 100)

14: POST MORTEM

Page 185 *Orthodoxy has at last caught up with me* Obituary published in *The Daily Express*, April 22, 1946

Page 186 *partly with a view to comparing* Memorandum from J.M. Keynes to the Estates Committee, King's College, Cambridge, May 8, 1938 (*CW, Vol. XII*, p. 102)

Page 186 *whence the satisfactory results came* Letter from J.M. Keynes to F.C. Scott, February 6, 1942 (*CW, Vol. XII*, p. 83)

Page 188 *I find Governing Bodies meetings* Letter from Lord Quickswood, Provost of Eton, to J.M. Keynes, December 17, 1943 (*CW, Vol. XII*, pp. 112–113)

Page 188 *All orthodox suggestions are too expensive* Letter from J.M. Keynes to R.E. Marsden, Bursar of Eton, March 8, 1944 (*CW, Vol. XII*, p. 111)

Page 189 *[Keynes] was an extremely active* Moggridge, (ed.), *Economic Articles and Correspondence: Investment and Editorial (CW, Vol. XII)*, 1983, p. 51

Page 189 *gave a good thrashing* Memorandum from J.M. Keynes to the Provincial Insurance Company, March 7, 1938 (*CW, Vol. XII*, p. 97)

Page 189 *with around 80 percent by value* see Chambers, D., Dimson, E. & Foo, J., "Keynes the Stock Market Investor: A Quantitative Analysis", *Journal of Financial and Quantitative Analysis*, Vol. 50, No. 4 (2015) which notes that "across the entire period [from 1921 to 1946], 81% by value (and 65% by number) of [Keynes'] year-end personal holdings were also held by King's"

Page 190 *generated disappointing returns in the 1920s* Chambers, D. & Dimson, E., "John Maynard Keynes, Investment Innovator", *Journal of Economic Perspectives*, Vol. 27, No. 3 (2013)

Page 192 *he valued Austin Motor shares* Ibid.

Page 193 *The more directly under Keynes' control* Skidelsky, *John Maynard Keynes: Fighting for Britain 1937–1946* (Volume 3), p. 524

Page 194 *Whereas in the 1920s Keynes was generally* Moggridge, *Maynard Keynes: An Economist's Biography*, p. 585

Page 194 *the avoidance of "stumers" with which* Letter from J.M. Keynes to F.C. Scott, June 7, 1938 (*CW, Vol. XII*, p. 66)

Page 194 *there had scarcely been a single case* Letter from J.M. Keynes to F.C. Scott, February 6, 1942 (*CW, Vol. XII*, p. 83)

Page 194 *The really dreadful losses* Graham, *The Intelligent Investor*, p. 8

Page 195 *one-armed contrarian who bought* Skousen, M., "Keynes as a Speculator: A Critique of Keynesian Investment Theory," in *Dissent on Keynes*, Praeger, New York, 1992, p. 166

Page 195 *One may be, and no doubt is* Letter from J.M. Keynes to R. F. Kahn, May 5, 1938 (*CW, Vol. XII*, p. 101)

Page 196 *not merely a maintenance of the present* Speech by J.M. Keynes at the Annual Meeting of National Mutual unit holders, February 19, 1936 (*CW, Vol. XXI*, p. 378)

Page 196 *I made a big mistake in not selling* Buffett, W., 2003 Chairman's Letter, February 27, 2004

Page 196 *If you stick with stocks that are underpriced* Comments by Charles Munger at the 2000 Berkshire Hathaway annual meeting

Page 196 *Maynard's judgment would have been* Bell, *Old Friends*, pp. 45–46

15: A SUMMING UP

Page 198 *I believe now that successful investment* Memorandum from J.M. Keynes to the Estates Committee, King's College, Cambridge, May 8, 1938 (*CW, Vol. XII*, pp. 106–107)

Page 198 *He was a Parliamentary Orator* Obituary published in *the New York Times*, April 22, 1946

Page 200 *It's a little like spending eight years* Buffett,W., transcript of a meeting of the New York Society of Financial Analysts, December 6, 1994

Page 200 *ramify ... into every corner of our minds* Keynes, J.M., Preface to *The General Theory of Employment, Interest and Money*, p. xxiii

Page 201 *[Mr Market] has incurable emotional problems* Buffett, W., 1987 Chairman's Letter, February 29, 1988

Page 201 *waves of irrational psychology* Keynes, J.M., *The General Theory of Employment, Interest and Money*, p. 162

Page 201 *Ships will sail around the world* Buffett, W., "The Superinvestors of Graham-and-Doddsville," *Hermes*, Fall 1984

Page 203 *[u]p until the 1960s prices were around twice as volatile* Haldane, A. "Patience and Finance", Oxford China Business Forum, Beijing, 9 September 2010

Page 204 *almost unlimited ability to ignore our ignorance* Kahneman, D., *Thinking, Fast and Slow*, Penguin Books, 2011, p. 201

Page 204 *Though markets are generally rational* Buffett, W., 2017, Chairman's Letter, February 24, 2018

Page 205 *we wait for extreme situations* Grantham, J., GMO Investment Letter, July 27, 2009

Page 206 *£20 million, or around $25 million, in 2019* Chambers, D., Dimson, E. & Spaenjers, C., "Art as an Asset: Evidence from Keynes the Collector", *Review of Asset Pricing Studies*, Vol. 10, No. 3 (2020), pp. 501, Table 3

Page 206 *[t]he collection performed especially well shortly after purchase* Ibid., p. 504

Page 206 *only 4 percent of U.S. stocks accounted for* see Bessembinder, H., "Wealth Creation in the U.S. Public Stock Markets 1926 to 2019"

Page 207 *The goal of the non-professional should not be to pick winners* Buffett, W., 2013 Chairman's Letter, February 28, 2014

Page 208 *Chambers and Dimson found that the Discretionary Portfolio* see Chambers, D. & Dimson, E., "John Maynard Keynes, Investment Innovator", *Journal of Economic Perspectives*

Page 208 *even the more innovative American university portfolios* see Chambers, D., Dimson, E. & Foo, J., "Keynes the Stock Market Investor: A Quantitative Analysis", *Journal of Financial and Quantitative Analysis*, Vol. 50, No. 4 (2015)

Page 208 *expect to have their decisions scrutinized* Kahneman, D., *Thinking, Fast and Slow*, Penguin Books, 2011 (p. 204)

Page 208 *even the more innovative American university portfolios* see Chambers, D., Dimson, E. & Foo, J., "Keynes the Stock Market Investor: A Quantitative Analysis"

Page 209 *Well here am I, like a recurring decimal* J.M. Keynes, quoted in Skidelsky, *John Maynard Keynes: Fighting for Britain 1937–1946* (Volume 3), p. 135

Page 209 *a sort of roving commission* Ibid., p. 79

Page 209 *Keynes must be one of the most* Howson and Moggridge (eds), *The Wartime Diaries of Lionel Robbins and James Meade*, pp. 158–159

Page 210 *he could be silent* Keynes, J.M., obituary for Sir Frederick Phillips, August 13, 1943 (*CW, Vol.* X, p. 330)

Page 210 *go for each other in a strident duet* Howson and Moggridge (eds), *The Wartime Diaries of Lionel Robbins and James Meade*, p. 135 (see also *CW, Vol. XXV*, p. 364)

Page 211 *for the cause as certainly* Robbins, L., "John Maynard Keynes: Profound Influence on Thought and Policy," *The Times*, January 26, 1951, p. 7

Page 212 *Progress is a soiled creed* Keynes, J.M., "The Underlying Principles," *Manchester Guardian Commercial*, January 4, 1923 (*CW, Vol. XVII*, p. 448)

Page 212 *I wish I had drunk more champagne* George Rylands, the British theater director and scholar, recalled that just a few months before he died, Keynes "voiced his one regret that he had not drunk more champagne in his life" (see Keynes, Milo [ed.]), *Essays on John Maynard* Keynes, p. 48)

Page 212 *Professors Chambers and Dimson found that* Dimson, E. "John Maynard Keynes, Investment Innovator", *Journal of Economic Perspectives*

INDEX

Note: JMK refers to John Maynard Keynes

ACKNOWLEDGEMENTS

Maynard Keynes once observed that his creative thinking generally began as a "grey, fuzzy, woolly monster" in his head. Only falteringly, and with much effort, were these thoughts given some semblance of shape and sense. In the process of writing this book, and wrestling with my own particular species of woolly monster, I have built up substantial debts of gratitude to many people. In particular, I would like to thank Professor David Chambers of the University of Cambridge's Judge Business School for his comments on the manuscript, the team at Black Inc. for their enthusiasm and professionalism, and my agent Jeanne Ryckmans for her support and infinite wisdom. Finally, I reserve my most heartfelt thanks and appreciation to my family for giving me the breathing space to indulge my own – possibly irrational – fascination with Keynes and the stock market.

ABOUT THE AUTHOR

Justyn Walsh is a former investment banker and corporate lawyer, and has worked across Europe, Asia, the Middle East and Australia. He is the CEO of an asset management firm and a company director.